WHEN PEOPLE
YOU TRUST
LET YOU DOWN

Experiencing God's
Faithfulness

WHEN PEOPLE YOU TRUST LET YOU DOWN

LARRY RICHARDS

WORD BOOKS
PUBLISHER
WACO, TEXAS

A DIVISION OF
WORD, INCORPORATED

WHEN PEOPLE YOU TRUST LET YOU DOWN:
EXPERIENCING GOD'S FAITHFULNESS

Unless otherwise indicated, Scripture quotations in this book are
from The Holy Bible, New International Version (NIV). Copyright
© 1973, 1978, 1984 International Bible Society. Used by permission of Zondervan Bible Publishers. Scripture marked KJV is from
the King James Version of the Bible.

Library of Congress Cataloging-in-Publication Data:

Richards, Larry, 1931–
      When people you trust let you down : experiencing God's
   faithfulness / Larry Richards.
         p.   cm.
      ISBN 0-8499-0529-X
      1. Interpersonal relations—Religious aspects—Christianity.
   2. Trust in God.   I. Title.
   BV4509.5.R49 1988
   248.4—dc19
                                                    88-10681
                                                       CIP

Printed in the United States of America

7 8 9 8   RRD   9 8 7 6 5 4 3 2 1

This series is for Sue

Hear my voice when I call, O Lord;
  be merciful to me and answer me.
My heart says of you, "Seek his face!"
  Your face, Lord, I will seek.
Do not hide your face from me,
  do not turn your servant away in anger;
  you have been my helper.
Do not reject me or forsake me,
  O God my Savior.
Though my father and mother forsake me,
  the Lord will receive me.

I am still confident of this:
  I will see the goodness of the Lord
  in the land of the living.
Wait for the Lord;
  be strong and take heart
  and wait for the Lord.

Psalm 27:7–10, 13–14

Contents

A Personal Word

God created us with a need for others. We need the warmth, the love, the security that are found only in sharing.

We need to share laughter.

To share love.

To share fears and sorrows and disappointments.

To share hopes and joys.

The need for a network of close, loving relationships is tightly woven into our very humanity. God has made us with a need to share ourselves with one another.

But sharing is filled with risk—especially these days, when dishonesty and betrayal seem rampant. Dare we trust others enough to invite them into our lives? How can we trust, when those we've trusted in the past have let us down?

David, the psalmist, knew the pain of trust betrayed. People for whom David had risked his life joined a plot to kill him. The love of David's wife turned to hatred and contempt. The nation David had led for a quarter century revolted against him, and it was David's own son who led that civil war!

Yet in Psalm 27 David says,

> I am still confident of this:
>   I will see the goodness of the Lord
>   in the land of the living.

This book is written for a time when someone you've trusted has let you down. It's written honestly, to do justice to the pain. But it is also written in the confidence that, no matter how deeply you have been hurt, you too can see the goodness of the Lord in the land of the living.

Each chapter is an independent meditation. Each is an invitation to see your hurt in fresh perspective. And each provides guidelines to help you reach out, to rebuild your capacity to trust.

I hope you'll want to share *When People You Trust Let You Down* with Christian friends. The questions at the end of each chapter ("For Meditation or Discussion") will help you use this book in a Sunday school class or with a group of people meeting at home. The experiences you discuss together, with the insights God gives each of you into his Word, can be a significant source of help.

But most important, this book is for you personally. It's written for times you are hurt by someone you trust—to bring healing, and to help you reach out and trust again. When others hurt you (as others have hurt me), may God bless you with a comforting sense of his faithfulness . . . and with the confidence that you too will see the goodness of the Lord in this, the land of the living.

Larry Richards

WHEN
PEOPLE
YOU TRUST
LET YOU
DOWN

1

God's
Fragile Gift

Sue reached out her hand to her husband.
"I'm afraid.
"I want to go home."
She looked so pale and vulnerable lying there on the hospital cart, waiting.

It had begun in August, her first day back at school after the summer vacation. Sue was piling books on the wall-mounted desk in her English Department office when suddenly the desk just fell away from the wall. Startled, Sue grabbed it—and felt a terrible pain in her lower back.

Sue didn't know it then, but the falling desk, which was supposed to have been fastened securely, had ruptured a disk in her spine.

Over the next months Sue experienced intermittent pain, but the chiropractor reassured her. Muscles had been pulled when the desk fell. Probably with adjustment and some physical therapy . . . well, it would be all right. But the pain persisted.

She took a powerful medication to reduce inflammation. And the pills *did* relieve the pain, but they also ate away her stomach lining. Sue developed a peptic ulcer.

She turned to the school administrators. No one suggested what to do next, or even seemed willing to help. What hurt was that Sue had thought of several administrators as friends. Now she felt abandoned. They didn't care about her, after all.

Finally Sue got an OK from the school's insurance company to get a second opinion. The company made an appointment with an orthopedic surgeon. But one of Sue's friends had heard of the doctor. "He's a butcher," Marge told Sue. "He had to join another practice because he couldn't even get malpractice insurance."

Panicked, Sue asked for a different doctor, but her insurance company insisted on the one they had picked. Surely, they said, it wouldn't hurt just to get his opinion.

She saw the doctor. He ordered a CAT scan and gave her a powerful muscle relaxant to relieve the muscle spasms that now were gripping her back so tightly she had trouble sleeping. When Sue got home, she glanced at the ingredients in the medicine. Along with the relaxant, those pills contained 750 grams of aspirin and 600 of caffeine—potentially deadly to a woman with an ulcer. And Sue had told the doctor all about her ulcer! How could she trust a physician who prescribed a medicine that was devastating to a condition they had thoroughly discussed?

No wonder that now, five months after her back had been injured, lying on the hospital cart and waiting for another doctor to work on her ruptured disk, Sue was afraid. How could she trust anyone?

The maintenance man responsible for fastening the desks into the wall had simply propped hers up and left it—an accident waiting to happen.

The school administrators she'd thought cared about her as a person had ignored or dismissed her pain.

The chiropractor had misdiagnosed her problem and suggested pain pills that gave her an ulcer.

The insurance company had sent her to an incompetent doctor.

And through it all, Sue was the one who had paid, in pain, the price of their failures. She had trusted each one. And each one had let her down.

How could she trust anyone now?

Sue's experience isn't all that unusual. Jim and Karen had been impressed by Carl Bowen, a man they knew only as their neighbor's financial counselor.

They'd been invited to Carl's five-hundred-thousand-dollar seacoast home with about a dozen other acquaintances. They'd been picked up by Carl's Mercedes limousine. The dinnerware was exquisite, the meal catered by the area's best restaurant. Afterward they'd all gone for a cruise on Carl's yacht to watch the sunset. Then their enthusiastic neighbors had told everyone of the great investments Carl had made for them. Modestly, Carl had shared some of the secrets of successful investing and had talked about two of the deals he was working on currently.

Jim and Karen were convinced. They cashed in their stocks, took their savings out of the bank, and gave everything to Carl.

Three months later they read that Carl Bowen had been arrested. Their money, and the money of others who had trusted him, was gone. Later, Jim and Karen ruefully told the local paper, "He seemed so successful."

Gen, too, had been fooled by appearances—at least, she felt she had been.

Gen lives on her social security check and the few dollars her daughter sends her. It isn't much, but it was enough for Gen. Enough to get by on—and enough to send small but regular checks to that television evangelist who seemed so sincere in his desire to help others.

Then the scandal came. Well, at first Gen wasn't taken in. Satan was just trying to smear one of God's servants.

But then the news stories kept rolling in—and Gen began to doubt. She thought about the money she'd sent—sent because that evangelist had made her feel the hurt of all those needy people in the world. How could he come on television and cry—cry real tears—if he didn't actually care?

At first Gen was angry. But then the anger went away, leaving her with nothing but an empty ache where her heart had been.

Kerri knows all about heartache. Her hurt hasn't come from figures seen only on a TV screen. Her hurt has flesh and blood. Her hurt has touched her, spoken to her daily, made love to her.

When Kerri wrote me, she'd been separated from her husband for only a few months. She wrote because, within a week of her leaving, he had become "religiously involved." He told Kerri he'd stopped his drinking, and she thought that might be true. But Kerri still wrote me, to ask if I thought she was bound to seek a reconciliation.

In her letter Kerri said, "My spouse has been untrue many times during our ten years together. My protests did not change his behavior. He has been abusive both physically and verbally. I have forgiven him over and over, but we have separated at times (usually following an episode of abuse). I have held on and prayed continually that the situation would be different. But my husband did not change, and I am not ready to expose the remainder of my children's formative years to the arguing and battering that were a constant part of this marriage.

"But am I bound to seek a reconciliation with this man now that he seems to have taken steps down the right road? I am referring not only to the infidelity, but to the fact that he has been quick-tempered, abusive in public, irresponsible with money decisions—and I know that I no longer love him. If we were together again, I'm afraid many of his old ways would surface."

Kerri's husband, the man she trusted to love and cherish her, violated that trust—violated it over and over again for ten long, pain-filled years. Now she says, "I gave myself and my life to him, and he hurt me irrevocably." No wonder Kerri no longer has the strength—or the desire—to trust him again.

It's so easy to tell stories about people who have suffered because someone they trusted has let them down.

I could tell you about Mario, who lives and works near Washington, D.C. Mario has been a good son to his aging parents. He's worked hard to help them. But Mario has just been cut out of his parents' will. Everything has been left to a sister who is never there. It really isn't the money, Mario says. It's the rejection that hurts.

I could tell about Stephen Breuning, a psychologist whose research at the University of Pittsburgh was very influential in certain areas of mental-health care. Several years ago Breuning was barred from further research when a panel of specialists determined that he had reported experiments he never carried out and reported results his experiments never obtained. How many ill persons have suffered because a researcher that the medical community trusted simply fabricated studies he never carried out?[1]

---

1. Daniel Greenberg, "Publish or perish—or fake it," *U.S. News & World Report*, 8 June 1987, pp.72–73.

I could tell you about Estelle. She's the wife of a well-known judge in Phoenix. Estelle was shaken when she learned her husband had been unfaithful. But she was shattered when he took her out to dinner and told her that he loves her and wants to remain married, but that he firmly intends to keep his young mistress too.

I could tell you about the respected young Dallas pastor whose congregation was totally stunned when he was arrested, tried, and convicted of tying up and humiliating several women who were complete strangers to him.

I could tell you the story of Ellen, whose best friend no longer sees her, but now gossips and laughs about personal things that Ellen shared with her in confidence.

Each of these stories is true. Each communicates something of the pain that comes when someone you trust lets you down.

It truly does hurt.

In some ways, there's no greater pain we can know.

Trust is such a fragile thing. When trust is broken, sharp fragments seem to penetrate our very hearts.

Yet the people we come to trust are also God's gift to us. This may be a fragile gift, but it is a great and vital one. We begin to sense its importance in the Creation story.

God had made Adam in his own image and placed him in a Garden the Lord himself prepared. There Adam's days were filled with delight. There was beauty to enjoy. There was satisfying labor in caring for the Garden. There was the excitement of discovery as Adam watched the creatures who shared Eden with him. And there was God, who often walked with Adam in the cool of the evening. But as the months and years passed, Adam experienced a strange disquiet, an unexplained emptiness.

Genesis says, "but for Adam no suitable helper was found" (Gen. 2:20).

The Hebrew word translated "helper" here means a help, a support. It does not imply an inferior, for God himself is cast in Scripture as man's helper in all kinds of distress. It simply implies that Adam alone was inadequate and unfulfilled.

And so God said, "It is not good for man to be alone. I will make a helper suitable for him" (Gen. 2:18).

It's true, of course, that the helper God gave to Adam was Eve. It is just as true that Adam was a gift to her. But while the focus of this passage is on the first pair, and its teaching is usually applied to marriage, much more is implied.

God, who created Adam and Eve, told them "be fruitful and increase in number; fill the earth" (Gen. 1:28). In Eve, God gave Adam more than a single companion; he gave him the potential to generate hundreds, thousands, millions of other human beings! God gave the first pair the potential of filling Earth with "suitable helpers."

So those words, "It is not good for man to be alone," suggest more than the intimacy of marriage. They imply the vast networks of interdependence that create and support civilizations!

Think about it for a moment.

Think how desperately we need suitable helpers. We need the medical researchers who have extended our lifespans with miracle drugs. We need the engineers who have created the wonders that warm and cool our homes, cook our meals, and let us travel thousands of miles in mere hours. We need the farmers who raise our food, the truckers who transport it. We need the teachers who educate us, the publishers who print our books. We need the plumbers who fix our sinks and the mechanics who repair our cars. We need the politicians who govern, the police who protect us. We need the pastors who minister to us, the friends who laugh and cry with us. We need the husband or wife who shares our most intimate moments. And we need the children who carry our hopes into the future.

All this was in the mind of God when he said, "It is not good for man to be alone."

All this was implicit in the one gift to Adam of Eve, when God said, "I will make a helper suitable for him."

True, those people God intended to be helpers do fail us. The healers sometimes harm, as Sue has been harmed. Some mechanics charge for repairs they didn't make. Some politicians prove to be venial or corrupt. Some of the police resell confiscated drugs. Some ministers betray their calling for money. All too many husbands and wives are unfaithful; too many parents are abusive; too many children rebel.

And yet . . .

And yet, we have to trust.

We do need others.

We dare not cut ourselves off because of hurt or because of the fear of being hurt again. Scripture's verdict remains true.

It isn't good for man to be alone.

Each of us needs to reach out to find the "suitable helpers" that God has prepared just for us. And each of us can—if we'll only pause to consider:

(1) *Despite our hurt, God has already given us suitable helpers.* When someone you trust lets you down, that experience can color your outlook on life. You can become bitter. You can withdraw or become depressed. Yet even when the pain is greatest, God invites you and me to maintain a positive outlook.

Paul wrote to the Philippians, "Finally, brothers, whatever is true, whatever is noble, whatever is right, whatever is pure, whatever is lovely, whatever is admirable—if anything is excellent or praiseworthy—think about such things" (Phil. 4:8).

This verse doesn't mean we should ignore our hurts or act as if they aren't important. God doesn't expect us to pretend. But when we look at things honestly, we have to admit that we have had positive experiences as well as negative ones. Some of those we've trusted really did care for us. Some have been our helpers—gifts from God who have enriched our lives.

God's call to think on the excellent and praiseworthy is intended to help keep us in touch with this reality. Yes, people we trust do let us down—but not *everyone*. And when life seems darkest, thinking about the blessings God has brought into our lives through other people can bring a comforting ray of hope.

(2) *Despite our hurt, God himself remains faithful.* One of David's psalms celebrates this certainty, even though David too was deeply hurt by those he trusted. The love of David's wife, Michal, had turned to contempt. The people David had ruled for decades had rebelled against him, and his own son, Absalom, had led the rebels in the civil war.

And yet David celebrated God's faithfulness. David knew that "though my father and mother forsake me, the Lord will receive me" (Ps. 27:10). In his troubles David did turn to God.

This same psalm shares the secret of David's confidence. Verse 4 says, "One thing I ask of the Lord, this is what I seek: that I may dwell in the house of the Lord all the days of my life, to gaze upon the beauty of the Lord and to seek him in his temple." God was no stranger to David. David's love for God, nurtured by time spent in worship and contemplation, was now a source of healing in his pain.

How good to know that you and I, too, are invited to love God, to spend time with him, and to contemplate his beauty. As you experience the faithfulness of God through his personal touch within, you too will find healing and strength.

(3) *Despite our hurt, the future is bright.* God has peopled our world with billions of living human beings. Among them is the person or persons you need, a person or persons you can trust who won't let you down. God, who said, "It is not good for man to be alone," has no intention of leaving you alone and lonely.

With David, you too can say, "I am still confident of this: I will see the goodness of the Lord in the land of the living" (Ps. 27:13).

For Meditation or Discussion

1. What has been most painful to you when someone you trusted let you down? How have you reacted up to this time? How have others you know felt when someone violated their trust?

2. Make a list of people you have trusted who *haven't* let you down. What has each contributed to your life? Make it a practice when you feel down to think about one of them and thank God for his or her contribution.

3. Read Psalm 27 thoughtfully. What in the psalm tells you something about David's disappointments? What tells you about his relationship with God? What explains his apparent positive attitude and hope?

4. One of the great values of the psalms is that they provide model prayers. What portion(s) of Psalm 27 do you want to express to God as your own prayer?

2

**Feet of
Clay**

I can see him now—backed up against the piano, his sharp, narrow face grinning, his bagpipe imitation punctuated every few moments by a vigorous bang on the keys with his rump. And all of us, adults and young people alike, almost helpless with laughter.

I have many images of him.

I remember a sermon he preached on Namaan the leper. It was at the closing program for Vacation Bible School the July I was twenty-one. I was in the Navy then, at a base just a few blocks from the church, and I'd gotten permission to take mornings off and teach a class of third-grade boys—the same kids I taught in Sunday school.

He was so dynamic that evening. He acted out the story, roving away from the pulpit, wringing every bit of drama from it. We were all captivated, and afterwards the adults joked and said it was the best sermon he'd ever preached. But what I remember is little Eddie Ranucci raising his hand at the invitation to show he was ready to receive Christ as Savior . . . and then turning to the boy next to him and saying, "Wouldn't you like to do what I just did?"

Those years in the Navy were some of the richest in my life. I had been brought up in a Christian home, but it wasn't until I had been in the Navy for two years that I made a conscious, personal commitment to Jesus. After that, I started to study my Bible intensely and even began to teach myself Greek. For six months I holed up at my base in Brooklyn, New York, reading the Bible and theology books and memorizing Scripture. I began a small lunch-hour Bible study. And then I began looking for a church. What I found was a little Baptist church on Bay Ridge Avenue. And Pastor L.

I can't begin to share what that church, its active young people's group, and especially Pastor L, meant to me. But I can share some of the memories—like the first time I went to a street meeting up at old Sunset Park.

We had an American flag, a trombone, an accordion, loud voices, and of course Pastor L. After a small crowd had gathered, he preached a five-minute sermon, and then I heard him say, "Larry, come here and tell these folks what Jesus Christ means to you!"

I haven't the slightest idea what I said. But I remember the drunk who peered owlishly at me, the kids on the fringes of the crowd who threw pebbles, the police car that cruised slowly by again and again, either protecting our rights or making sure we didn't start a riot. That was the first time I had ever publicly given witness to Jesus.

Pastor L was like that. He made sure that our faith wasn't just of the Sunday-go-to-meeting stripe.

Even young people had an active role to play in that little church. The youth group, whose ages ranged from thirteen to twenty-four, conducted services at three New York rescue missions each month. We were responsible, under a deacon, for the annual two-week revival meetings held each summer. We launched and coordinated cottage prayer meetings for the services, and we put on a banquet that concluded them. We even collected the money and took a "love offering" for the evangelist.

For me, though, there was even more. In the Navy I felt God was calling me to the ministry. Pastor L made sure I had opportunities to understand what was involved.

I remember the first time I spent the day with him. We started off by driving to one of the hospitals a few miles away. On the way, Pastor L told me about the man we were going to visit. He was an alcoholic who had often "accepted Christ" but couldn't break the hold of drink. This time he'd been lying in a gutter when a truck had come along and run over both his legs.

"Larry," Pastor L said as we entered the hospital, "you pick a scripture to read, and I'll pray with him."

All I could think of was a passage I'd been reading that morning. So I stood by the man's bed and read from the Gospel of John, chapter 9. As we drove to the next place, Pastor L told me I'd made a good choice and explained why.

Then we went to a home where a seven-year-old was dying of cancer. Pastor L told me that the child and the mom were Christians. The dad had promised God to believe, if only his son got well. But now it was only a matter of days, and the father was bitter and angry.

"Larry," Pastor L said as we went up to the door, "I'll read Scripture, and you pray with them."

Oh yes. I have so many memories of those days—and of my mentor, Pastor L.

One of my most vivid memories is of the shock when one day he simply walked out on his wife, his two teenaged children, and his church.

The only report of him that I've heard in over thirty years now is that he was seen laughing and chatting in a

restaurant in Canada, accompanied by an attractive
young woman whom people thought was his wife.

What can we do when we discover that the Christian
leaders we admire have feet of clay? Certainly that's a
discovery many of us are making these days.

The president of one theological seminary called
1987 "the year of the evangelical scandals." In a letter to
friends of the seminary, he wrote, "Hardly a week goes
by that I don't hear of a ministry or church caught in
turmoil. The crisis often involves leadership issues, and
frequently moral impurity is the problem."

I don't want to be another of those who keep scandal
on the front page just to titillate readers. And I don't
want to join the judges who so quickly condemn Christian brothers and sisters, often before all the facts are
known. But if we are to deal with hurt that comes when
Christian leaders we trust let us down, we need to look
briefly at just two documented cases of ministerial
scandal.

Gordon MacDonald, the author of several helpful
Christian books, was president of InterVarsity Christian
Fellowship. But on 5 June 1987, IVCF headquarters is-
sued a news release. President MacDonald was resigning
"for personal reasons, having been involved in an adul-
terous relationship in late 1984 and early 1985."

Courageously, MacDonald told the story in his own
words in the 10 July 1987 issue of *Christianity Today*. An
editorial by Verne Becker in InterVarsity's magazine for
college youth summarizes:

> Gordon ended the affair, repented and confessed the
> sin to God and to several Christian leaders privately,
> submitting himself to their discipline. They advised him
> to slow down his schedule and outside commitments,

but didn't feel the need to make the affair public. Late this past spring, however, anonymous letters disclosing the affair were sent to various Christian publishers, and Gordon decided to step down to avoid damaging Inter-Varsity's reputation.

The things MacDonald did to deal with his sin were responsible Christian acts. But still the editorial writer shares, "the whole thing shocked me. When I heard it, I felt the blood drain from my body." The same writer shares the reaction of friends, many of them college students involved with IVCF: "If *he* can give in to temptation, what hope is there for *me?*"[1]

Then there's the case of Jim and Tammy Faye Bakker. Jim's problems became public when another minister accused him of homosexual liaisons and of having a brief affair with a church secretary, procured for him by yet another preacher. Later the public learned that the church secretary, who has been variously cast as a betrayed innocent and a manipulative former prostitute, was being paid for her silence from a fund set up with donations given to PTL, Jim's Christian TV network.

When Jim resigned and turned his network over to another TV preacher, his finances were revealed. Jim and Tammy and top network officers had been skimming millions from the donations given by their viewers. They had bought palatial homes and luxury cars and had paid themselves million-dollar salaries—all this while pleading poverty and begging for just a few dollars more from the faithful to support the "ministries."

Overnight "PTL" lost its intended significance as "Praise the Lord" or "People that Love." In the popular mind PTL became "Pass the Loot," or "Pay the Lady!"

---

1. Verne Becker, "When a Hero Falls," *U*, October 1987, p. 32.

A syndicated column by Tom Wicker, which appeared about the time of the PTL scandal, reports just a few of the excesses of the Bakkers, which have been documented from financial records:

- In 1986, of PTL's $129 million in revenues . . . only 2.9 percent went to charitable programs.
- That year, most of the organization's overseas "missions" were discontinued so that PTL could pay bills for Heritage USA, its "Christian theme park" at Fort Mill, South Carolina.
- But also in 1986, the Bakkers themselves collected $1.6 million in salaries and bonuses.
- In the first three months of 1987, salaries and bonuses to Jim Bakker and his top assistants exceeded $1 million; the Bakkers together received $480,000 compensation during one 10-day stretch in February.

After giving the facts, Wicker comments,

> The real depravity of all this is not in the figures alone. It's rather in the fact that these huge sums were obtained mostly in small amounts from honest, believing Americans, many of them poor as Job's turkey, who in the Christian spirit of mission and sacrifice sent in their mite for what they believed was the propagation of the faith.[2]

To date there's no report of a public confession from the Bakkers like the one from Gordon MacDonald. They did however set up a 900 number with the phone company where the faithful, for a small fee billed by AT&T, could get daily updates on Jim and Tammy's side of the story.

And then there was the "Goodbye for Now" concert

---

2. Tom Wicker, "A Ministry of Loot," *The New York Times*, 30 May 1987, p. 31.

tour that a promoter booked cross-country. That was canceled when the first dates, in auditoriums built for thousands, presold a few dozen tickets at most.

The last I heard was that a local church somewhere had reordained Jim Bakker to the ministry. His own denomination had revoked his ministerial credentials.

But what about all those people who gave because they *are* people that love? What about all those people who cried too when Tammy or Jim wept on the set? What about the "partners" who pledged and gave at least a thousand dollars to PTL? What happens to folks like these when the ministers they trust let them down?

It happened to me with Pastor L.

It happened to hundreds of students with Gordon MacDonald.

It happened to hundreds of thousands with Jim and Tammy Faye Bakker.

And perhaps it's happened to you. Perhaps you were let down by a minister or a spiritual advisor you trusted.

When it does happen, what can we do?

Whatever can we *do?*

Two lines of teaching in Scripture may help us put such experiences in perspective.

The first is summed up in Jeremiah's warning: "Cursed is the one who trusts in man, who depends on flesh for his strength" (Jer. 17:5). The Hebrew word translated "curse" means a "solemn warning." It is often used in Scripture to make people aware ahead of time of judgments that must follow actions which God condemns. Here the meaning is clear: we cannot ultimately depend on any human hero.

Mankind is just flesh and blood. We are all weak and vulnerable. Not one person in this world besides Jesus has ever lived without sinning. Not one person besides Jesus could ever be *totally* depended on.

Yet Jeremiah goes on. Though he warns us against depending too much on other human beings, he pronounces a special blessing on those who look beyond people to God. "But blessed is the man who trusts in the Lord, whose confidence is in him" (Jer. 17:7). If we put our real trust in God and not his human representatives, the shattering of their feet of clay will never shake our faith.

The other line of teaching is found in what the Bible has to say about "false teachers." Not everyone who claims to speak for God does so. Some speak falsely. Several passages in Scripture deal with counterfeit ministers. One of the most complete treatments is found in 2 Peter 2.

Peter, writing about false prophets of Old Testament times, says, "there will [also] be false teachers among you" (v. 1). And he goes on to give several signs by which false teachers can be recognized. Such people introduce "destructive heresies," and their own "shameful [immoral] ways will bring the truth into disrepute." Furthermore, "in their greed these teachers will exploit you with stories they have made up" (vv. 1–3).

These counterfeit ministers "follow the corrupt desire of the sinful nature and despise authority" (v. 10). Their "idea of pleasure is to carouse in broad daylight." They "revel in their pleasures while they feast with you." And, "with eyes full of adultery, they never stop sinning; they seduce the unstable; they are experts in greed" (vv. 13–14).

The chapter concludes, "they mouth empty, boastful words and, by appealing to the lustful desire of sinful human nature, they entice people. . . . They promise them freedom, while they themselves are slaves of depravity" (vv. 18–19).

The points made by Peter are also found in 2 Timothy

and in Jude. Initially false teachers seem attractive, for they do counterfeit godliness. But in time their character is revealed in characteristics for which Christians must watch. These are:

- *Signs in their characters:* False teachers are arrogant. They refuse to submit to the authority of others or to be accountable to others (Jer. 23:10; 2 Pet. 2:10; Jude 16). They are motivated by the desires of the sinful nature, which may find expression as immorality or pride (Jer. 23:14; 2 Pet. 2:10; Jude 4, 19). They have a love for wealth and use the ministry to make money (2 Pet. 2:15; Jude 12).
- *Signs in their ministry:* Their ministry appeals to the "lustful desires of the human nature" (Jer. 23:14b; 2 Pet. 2:18; Jude 16). They promise things that naturally appeal to human nature. And their ministry promises "freedom" (Jer. 23:16–17; 2 Pet. 2:19). This promise of freedom may involve release from moral restraints, but may be a promise of release from the physical, financial, or other limitations under which individuals may be called to live.

We can't expect to see all these signs fully developed in the life or ministry of any spiritual leader we are encouraged to trust. But there will be clues—clues which Scripture identifies so that we might be warned and might look instead for the qualities which do mark a godly leader.

When a spiritual leader we have trusted fails us, then, it may be for one of at least two reasons. We may have trusted a false teacher, one of Satan's counterfeits. Or we may have trusted the right person but not realized

that he or she is just a person like you and me. We may
have trusted a person whose failure simply proves his
humanity and who now deserves our compassion and our
prayers.

In either case, there are several things that we can
learn when our spiritual heroes prove to have feet of clay:

(1) *Use discernment in deciding whom to trust.* The
Bible doesn't list characteristics of false teachers so that
we can go about applying the label to this person or
that. The characteristics are listed so that we can be
warned—and learn not to extend trust too quickly.

The Bible also lists characteristics of *trustworthy*
leaders. Paul tells Timothy that a spiritual leader "must
be above reproach, the husband of but one wife, tem-
perate, self-controlled, respectable, hospitable, able to
teach, not given to drunkenness, not violent but gentle,
not quarrelsome, not a lover of money" (1 Tim. 3:2–3).
It is people like this, who also "keep hold of the deep
truths of the faith with a clear conscience," that we can
depend on to help us on our spiritual journey.

Yet as Paul says in this passage, there's another test
of trustworthy leadership. Those we entrust with leadership "must not be a recent convert." Anyone to be con-
sidered for leadership "must first be tested" [by time]
(vv. 6, 10).

Even when we do accept someone as a spiritual leader,
let's remember not to idealize him or her. That person is
very human, too, and has a special need for our prayers.
If he or she fails, and confesses the failure, then he or she
deserves our support, love, and forgiveness.

Yes, we need our spiritual heroes.

But ultimately our trust must be in God, not mere men.

(2) *Don't give up.* When a spiritual leader displays
feet of clay, we need not grow cynical or give up. When

a leader fails, it is not at all as though God's Word has failed.

In fact, the failure of leaders proves the truth of Scripture! It is the Word of God that Jesus states when he says to his disciples, "Apart from me you can do nothing" (John 15:5).

It is only when a leader—or a follower like you and I—stays in an intimate, obedient relationship with Jesus that we can be spiritually fruitful. Without constant reliance on Jesus, anyone is bound to fail.

(3) *Bless God for the blessings.* As I look back on my experience in Brooklyn, I thank God for Jesus' ministry to me through Pastor L. The tragedy isn't in what Pastor L's failure did to me or to others. The tragedy is in what Pastor L's failure did to him!

In 1 Corinthians 13, the Apostle Paul surveys the importance of love. He says in conclusion that, even if a person gives all, but has not love, he "gains nothing" (v. 3).

I've thought often about that verse. It's not that *others* fail to gain from a loveless ministry. It's the one who ministers who gains nothing.

So I do bless God for Pastor L, though I hurt for his family and the church he deserted. God used him in my life. I thank God for the rich gifts Jesus gave me through someone who even then may have been a tormented man.

I gained so much from Pastor L.

So, I suspect, did his family. His daughter is a missionary now, his son a respected Christian leader.

Yes, they were hurt.

But only one man was destroyed by the shattering of those human feet of clay.

Only one man gained . . . nothing.

For Meditation or Discussion

1. Have you ever been hurt when a person you looked up to as a spiritual leader let you down? Tell someone what happened. Share how you felt, and how the experience has affected you since.

2. Look at what Paul writes about Christian leaders in 1 Timothy 3 and Titus 1 and compare with the description of false teachers in 2 Peter 2 and Jude. What "little signs" might you look for to help you determine whom you would trust as a spiritual leader?

3. This chapter suggests that the person who suffers most from the failure of a Christian leader is that leader himself. If a leader you trusted has let you down, why not list all the positive blessings God has given you through him or her. Then thank the Lord for that ministry to you. Let thanksgiving comfort you, give you perspective, and heal the hurt. And then pray for the wounded leader.

3

Where Are the Wonders?

The Bible tells that in the days of the Judges an angel appeared to a young man named Gideon. The angel announced, "The Lord is with you, mighty warrior."

That was news to Gideon.

At the moment he was crouching in a secluded winepress, trying to separate a few kernels of wheat from their stalks.

This was usually done high on some hillside. The sheaves of grain were pounded to loosen the kernels and then tossed in the air. The wind would blow the chaff and stalks away, while the heavier kernels of grain fell to the ground.

But Gideon, crouching behind stone walls, was afraid to thresh his grain in the open. He was hiding, hoping that the aggressive Midianites who occupied Israel's territory wouldn't see him and take the grain away.

The Lord is with you?

Mighty warrior?

Sure.

Sometimes we imagine that the heroes of the Bible possessed some special, unique faith that ordinary people today lack. Things went well for them because they never, ever, doubted God.

Well, Gideon doesn't fit that notion. In fact, Gideon was a skeptic, honest enough to express doubt.

"But sir," Gideon replied, "if the Lord is with us, why has all this happened to us? Where are his wonders that our fathers told us about when they said, 'Did not the Lord bring us up out of Egypt?' But now the Lord has abandoned us and put us into the hand of Midian" (Judg. 6:13).

With these words Gideon expressed something that all of us feel at times. It's not just people we trust who let us down. At times God seems to let us down, too.

"Where are the wonders?" we can't help thinking.

"Why has all this happened to us?"

And, "Now even the Lord has abandoned us."

When we compare such feelings with Scripture, we realize that something doesn't quite fit. The Bible reveals a faithful God who simply does not let down the people who trust him.

That word, *faithful*, is special even in English. My dictionary defines it this way:

FAITH · FUL. 1. keeping faith; maintaining allegiance to someone or something; constant; loyal.

Biblical words translated "faithful" are even more powerful. In the Old Testament, for instance, the Hebrew words for faithful are drawn from one of the Bible's great theological terms, *'āman*. This Hebrew word is the root on which words like *truth, certainty, established,* and *support* are constructed.

Simply put, the Bible portrays God as a completely dependable Person, a Person who will never let down someone who trusts in him.

God's faithfulness is one of the established certainties in this uncertain universe. It is a truth which is in total and complete harmony with reality. God's faithfulness is one of those things which serves as a support to the believer in every one of life's situations.

Look at just a few of the biblical passages which affirm and celebrate God's faithfulness:

He is the Rock, his works are perfect,
   and all his ways are just.
A faithful God who does no wrong,
   upright and just is he (Deut. 32:4).

Sing to him a new song;
   play skillfully, and shout for joy.
For the word of the Lord is right and true;
   he is faithful in all he does (Ps. 33:3, 4).

Your love, O Lord, reaches to the heavens,
   your faithfulness to the skies (Ps. 36:5).

I will sing of the Lord's great love forever;
   with my mouth I will make your faithfulness known
   through all generations.
I will declare that your love stands firm forever,
   that you established your faithfulness in heaven
   itself. . . .
The heavens praise your wonders, O Lord,
   your faithfulness too, in the assembly of the holy
   ones. . . .
O Lord God Almighty, who is like you?
   You are mighty, O Lord, and your faithfulness
   surrounds you. . . .
Righteousness and justice are the foundation of
   your throne;
   love and faithfulness go before you (Ps. 89:1–2, 14).

In these and other passages, God's faithfulness is associated with other attributes. God is faithful. He is also righteous, upright, just, and loving. In his faithfulness to us, God is also faithful to righteousness. He is faithful to justice. He is faithful to love.

So what about Gideon's questions—and ours? What about those times when even God seems to have let us down?

The psalmist gives us a clue when he says,

> I know, O Lord, that your laws are righteous,
>   and in faithfulness you have afflicted me.
> May your unfailing love be my comfort,
>   according to your promise to your servant
>   (Ps. 119:75–76).

It may be hard to grasp, but even our greatest difficulties may demonstrate God's faithfulness.

If we return to Gideon for a moment, we can see this was true in his case. For his story is launched in Judges 6 with a report of Israel's idolatry. And we are told that God had even sent a prophet to explain that the oppression by the Midianites was God's punishment, because "you have not listened to me" (v. 6).

In other words, the oppression Gideon's people were experiencing actually was *proof* of God's faithfulness—a fulfillment of the promise he made through Moses to bless when his people obeyed him and to discipline when they disobeyed (Deut. 28).

But not every human tragedy is divine discipline.

Not every difficulty we experience is punishment.

All too often we have better grounds than Gideon to cry out, "Where are the wonders?" and to ask, "Why has all this happened to us?"

Job, the sufferer, shocked the religious men who had come to comfort him in his grief. These men were convinced that Job must have sinned terribly for God to permit such terrible things to happen to him.

But Job argued. He wasn't aware of any sins.

Finally Job was driven to say something that most of us know, but that many religious people are afraid to admit. Here, in brief paraphrase of chapter 21, are Job's observations on the unfairness of life:

"Listen! Listen, and then mock. But now listen and be surprised.

"You talk about the end of the wicked. Well, look around. We each know wicked men who do prosper. They get old. They see their grandchildren. Their houses are safe, nothing bad seems to happen to them.

"God doesn't use his rod on them. Why, they mock God! They say, 'Why serve God? We're doing all right without him. Where's the profit in prayer?'

"How often do folks like this really get what they deserve?

"Oh, you say, they get it in the end.

"But *when?* Why, God's children seem to suffer more than the ungodly!

"*Who* repays the wicked? Your answers are all lies."

All you and I have to do is to look around us to see that the wicked often prosper. In fact God's children seem to suffer more than the ungodly do.

It's no wonder that sometimes we feel God has let us down. It's no wonder that when suffering comes we may ask Gideon's questions, and with far more justification!

Lord, if you are faithful, where are the wonders?

Lord, if you are faithful, why has this happened to us?

Lord, if you are faithful, why have you abandoned us?

To gain perspective on our doubts, we need to remember something I noted earlier. In the Bible, God's
faithfulness is associated with his other attributes.

God is not simply faithful to *us*.

God is also faithful to his justice.

He is faithful to his righteousness.

He is faithful to his love.

Yes, God *is* faithful to us. But being faithful to us
doesn't mean that God always does what we think we
want. Being faithful means that God will express his
commitment to us within the framework established by
his own justice, righteousness, and love.

Put most simply, this means that God is *faithful to his
purpose for us*.

That purpose is expressed in the Bible in several different ways.

Jesus spoke of his followers as learners who, when
fully trained, would "be like" their Teacher (Luke 6:40).

Romans 8:29 says that those whom God has called are
destined "to be conformed to the likeness of his Son."

Second Corinthians 3:18 portrays God the Holy Spirit
actively at work within us, so that we "are being transformed into [Jesus'] likeness."

Colossians 3:10 speaks of a "new self" for the believer,
which "is being renewed in knowledge in the image of its
Creator."

The writer of Hebrews views the experiences we have
in this life as "discipline" (literally, "training"), and says
that while no discipline seems pleasant at the time, God's
discipline "produces a harvest of righteousness and peace
for those who have been trained by it" (Heb. 12:11).

Simply put, God's purpose for those he loves is growing up in godliness, becoming more and more Christlike.

This is something any parent should be able to understand.

Seven-year-old Sarah doesn't want to pick up her room.

Sarah wants to eat sweets, not meat and vegetables.

Sarah wants to watch TV instead of doing school work.

Sarah wants to stay up and watch a late movie instead of going to bed at nine.

Sarah wants to use lipstick and look "beautiful."

Sarah wants to buy some toy every time she goes to the store, and she's developed the habit of complaining constantly when her folks say no.

Sarah doesn't want to take the dishes out of the dishwasher or fold her clothes after her mom has washed them.

Sarah doesn't like the swat on the rump that her smart mouth sometimes earns.

Sarah doesn't want her friends to go home when their moms say it's time for supper.

Is Sarah a bad girl? Not at all! She's a healthy, normal, really nice seven-year-old. But if Sarah is to grow up to be a healthy, normal, really nice adult, her mom and dad know that Sarah mustn't get everything she wants so badly now.

Mom and Dad are faithful to Sarah, and to their purpose of helping her grow up well. And often their faithfulness is shown by *not* giving her what she thinks she wants. For a parent, being faithful can mean disappointing a child or even causing a child distress.

This is how you and I need to see God—as a loving parent so committed to us that he remains faithful to his purposes, and so faithful that he even permits us to hurt, so that good may grow out of our hurt.

Oh, I know.

Often, like Job, we can't see any good in our pain.

But then, Sarah has a hard time with many of the

decisions her mom and dad make that cause her pain. At seven, Sarah can't see why she has to do things she doesn't like—any more than we can grasp the reason for some of God's decisions concerning us.

But perhaps we don't really need to understand.

It may be enough to know that God is.

It may be enough to know that God loves us.

It may be enough to know that God is, truly is, faithful.

When we hurt and feel that the God we trusted has let us down, three truths can help us:

(1) *God is faithful in his purposes.* God thinks too much of us to let us have everything we want or think we need. God cares for us too much to insulate us from suffering. God has chosen to give us the greatest gift of all—we are to be like him and his Son, Jesus. And God remains faithful to that commitment.

This is, of course, the thought expressed in one of the Bible's most beloved verses, Romans 8:28: "We know that in all things God works for the good of those who love him, who have been called according to his purpose." That verse is incomplete without the next one, which states God's purpose: "For those God foreknew he also predestined to be conformed to the likeness of his Son."

So when we become discouraged and are tempted to ask, "Where are the wonders?" this verse gives us an answer.

The wonder is that God loves you and me so much that he has dedicated himself to make us like his Son.

(2) *God is faithful in his presence.* When Gideon assumed, "now the Lord has abandoned us," he was completely wrong. The oppression Israel was experiencing was actually proof that God had *not* abandoned his peo-

ple! If God didn't care, he would hardly have bothered to discipline them; he would simply have ignored them.

We need to remember this when pain makes us feel abandoned. God *does* care. And God is with us, even when we hurt the most.

God's words through Isaiah to people who lived some seven hundred years before Christ are intended just as much for you and me. Listen to his promise:

> But now, this is what the Lord says—
>   he who created you, O Jacob,
>   he who formed you, O Israel;
> "Fear not, for I have redeemed you;
>   I have called you by name; you are mine.
> When you pass through the waters,
>   I will be with you;
> and when you pass through the rivers,
>   they will not sweep over you.
> When you walk through the fire,
>   you will not be burned;
>   the flames will not set you ablaze.
> For I am the Lord, your God,
>   the Holy One of Israel, your Savior" (Isa. 43:1–3).

If God truly is your Savior, he will be faithful to you— always. And here is the wonder: When you pass through the waters of suffering, you will not be alone, for God says, "I will be with you."

(3) *God is faithful in his participation.* History provides the greatest proof that God is faithful even when we hurt. One day God sent his Son into our world. That Son, Jesus, subjected himself to all our limitations. He lived a life of poverty and self-sacrifice. Ultimately he suffered death on the cross so that you and I might be reconciled to God.

What history teaches us is that God did not stand back, an observer watching humankind experience pain. Instead, God became a participant in our humanity. And he did this that through his suffering you and I might be reconciled to God, transformed, and lifted up to glory.

Where are the wonders?

Here is the wonder upon wonder!

God was so committed to his purpose for us that he would not even spare himself.

When an occasion in our lives brings dark doubt and makes us question whether God too has let us down, how good it is to remember, God "did not spare his own Son, but gave him up for us all" (Rom. 8:32).

And we can be confident that everything God gives us—just like Jesus—will ultimately prove to be good.

For Meditation or Discussion

1. Share with someone an experience in which you felt that God had somehow let you down. Why did you feel that way? What did you think God should have done? Looking back, can you see any good that has come out of that experience?

2. Pick one of the verses on faithfulness quoted in this chapter to memorize. Or use a concordance to find another verse that is meaningful to you. Meditate on that verse when you experience unusual difficulty or pain.

3. This chapter states that God's faithfulness must be understood as faithfulness to God's purpose for us. What do you think that means? How might that concept have helped you deal with the experience you shared in response to question 1?

4

Betrayed

When the Catholic church was looking around for patron saints, I believe they missed an important one:

A patron saint for the sexually abused.

For the battered wife.

For the woman who trusted a man—and was betrayed.

Well, my candidate for that post is a well-known but much misunderstood woman. Bathsheba.

The biblical text takes great care to let us know that what happened to Bathsheba wasn't her fault. Look at the familiar story as it's told in 2 Samuel 11:

> In the spring, at the time when kings go off to war, David sent Joab out with the king's men and the whole Israelite army. They destroyed the Ammonites and besieged Rabbah. But David remained in Jerusalem.
>
> One evening David got up from his bed and walked around on the roof of the palace. From the roof he saw a woman bathing. The woman was very beautiful, and David sent someone to find out about her. The man said, "Isn't that Bathsheba, the daughter of Eliam and the wife of Uriah the Hittite?" Then David sent messengers to get her. She came to him, and he slept with her. Then she went back home. The woman conceived and sent word to David, saying, "I am pregnant" (vv. 1–5).

It happened "in the spring." In biblical days, spring wasn't the poet's season, when "a young man's fancy lightly turns to thoughts of love." Spring was the season when kings in the Middle East made war. But this year David, Israel's warrior king, stayed home. Staying home was out of character for David. It was also a violation of custom. David should have been with his troops.

David saw Bathsheba one evening after he "got up from his bed." Clearly Bathsheba hadn't planned to be seen; she was bathing after people were in bed. David would never have seen her if he hadn't been restless and unable to sleep that night.

David saw her when he "walked around on the roof of the palace." In biblical times, houses often were built with yards that were surrounded by walls but open to the sky. From his palace roof, David apparently looked down into one of these enclosed yards and saw Bathsheba bathing in what she supposed was complete privacy.

The text says Bathsheba "was very beautiful." The Hebrew language has two words used to describe attractive persons and things. One means simply "good looking." The other means "desirable." In the Hebrew, Bathsheba is called desirable.

It wasn't Bathsheba's fault. There's no reason to think she tried to arouse men's passions. But when David saw her, he was aroused.

So David sent someone to find out who this desirable woman was. And even after he learned that Bathsheba was the wife of one of his own army officers, he "sent messengers to get her." What could Bathsheba do? David was king. In ancient times, kings were obeyed—especially by a defenseless woman.

Bathsheba came to David.

And "he slept with her."

The story is told so simply in Scripture. The language is direct, the details few. Nothing is said of how used Bathsheba must have felt. Nothing is said of how shocked she must have been that David, a ruler with a reputation for loving God, could simply summon her, have sex with her, and send her away.

Nothing is said of her shame, her anger, her fears about how to face her husband when he returned. Nothing is said of how she must have hated her beauty then, and wished bitterly that she looked like an ordinary woman.

Nothing is said about how worthless she must have felt, not because she was worthless, but because she had been treated as a plaything rather than as a person to be valued and loved.

And this had been done to her by *David!*

The one person in Israel who seemed most worthy of trust had let Bathsheba down.

Oh yes. If you're looking for a patron saint for the betrayed, there's no need to look any further. It should be Bathsheba.

Bathsheba would understand.

One of the people Bathsheba would have understood is M'Liss Switzer. Brought up by an abusive older sister, M'Liss thought that meeting Chuck was the best thing that had ever happened to her.

They dated for fourteen months, and all that time Chuck was loving and supportive. Then, on their wedding night, when things didn't go just as Chuck had expected, he exploded, slapping M'Liss again and again.

Chuck apologized. But soon it became clear that such violence was going to be a pattern in their marriage.

In her book, *Called to Account*, M'Liss shares that whenever anything went wrong, whenever they

disagreed or she complained, "Chuck would explode
At his hands I suffered black eyes, broken eyeglasses,
bruises, twisted arms, pulled hair, sexual abuse, and
attempted stranglings."

In time, M'Liss began to feel that what was happening
was her fault—that Chuck's abuse was caused by her fail-
ings. And of course, her church warned her that there
could be no escape from the situation through divorce.

Bathsheba would have understood Kerri, too.

Kerri, whose letter I quoted in the first chapter of this
book, finally had enough after ten years of physical and
verbal abuse.

She had held on and prayed that the situation would
change. She had forgiven his infidelities over and over.

But finally, worried about exposing her children to
more years of constant arguing and battering, Kerri left,
saying, "I gave myself and my life to him and he hurt me
irrevocably."

Both these women, like hundreds of thousands of others today, know all too well what it is to be betrayed by
someone they thought they could trust.

I doubt that Bathsheba would tell Kerri she has to go
back to the husband who betrayed her, as all too many
folks demand these days.

Perhaps, instead, Bathsheba would just tell Kerri the
rest of her story.

When David learned that Bathsheba was pregnant,
he quickly recalled her husband. Uriah reported to the
king, but refused to sleep with his wife while his troops
were on the battlefield. A desperate David sent secret
orders to the commander of his armies. Uriah was to be
placed in an exposed position where he would be killed
by the enemy.

And so Bathsheba's husband died.

Then David took the pregnant Bathsheba into the palace and married her.

Nothing is said of whether Bathsheba wanted to marry this man who had used and betrayed her and then had arranged for the death of her husband. Nothing need be said. After all, David was king. Bathsheba had nothing to say—about anything.

Then, before the baby Bathsheba had conceived was born, the prophet Nathan confronted David and openly accused him.

Later, other kings of Israel would kill prophets who confronted them. Instead, David humbled himself. He confessed, "I have sinned." Not only did David confess to Nathan and to God, but because his actions had become public knowledge, David also made a public confession. He wrote a psalm, to be used in public worship, and the superscription of that psalm says, "when the prophet Nathan came to him after David had committed adultery with Bathsheba."

In that great psalm of confession, David acknowledges his sins. He appeals not only for forgiveness, but also for God to cleanse him and again give him a pure heart. Reading those words today, we can sense the depth of David's repentance:

> Have mercy on me, O God,
>   according to your unfailing love;
> according to your great compassion
>   blot out my transgressions.
> Wash away all my iniquity
>   and cleanse me from my sin.
> For I know my transgressions,
>   and my sin is always before me.
> Against you, you only, have I sinned
>   and done what is evil in your sight,

so that you are proved right when you speak
    and justified when you judge.
Surely I was sinful at birth,
    sinful from the time my mother conceived me.
Surely you desire truth in the inner parts;
    you teach me wisdom in the inmost place. . . .
Create in me a pure heart, O God,
    and renew a steadfast spirit within me.
Do not cast me from your presence
    or take your Holy Spirit from me.
Restore to me the joy of your salvation
    and grant me a willing spirit, to sustain me.
Then will I teach transgressors your ways,
    and sinners will turn back to you. . . .
The sacrifices of God are a broken spirit;
    a broken and contrite heart,
O God, you will not despise (Psalm 51:1–17).

After David repented, things changed for David and Bathsheba. The child they had conceived in adultery died, but the marriage of these two people, the woman who had been betrayed and the man who so cruelly betrayed her, survived!

First Chronicles 3 tells us that they had four sons together. Shammua. Shobab. Nathan (named in honor of the prophet who confronted David?). And Solomon, who succeeded David on Israel's throne.

The next time we meet Bathsheba, it is many years later. David is old, about to die. He has promised Bathsheba that their son Solomon will be the next king, but he has not made a public announcement. Another son of David, thinking his father too weakened by age to act, tries to grasp the throne himself. And Nathan the prophet hurries to enlist the help of the one person who can still influence David: Bathsheba.

The scene, described in 1 Kings 1, is touching. Bathsheba enters David's room and kneels down beside him. After their talk, Bathsheba slips away, and Nathan comes in to confirm her report. Moved by his desire to protect Bathsheba, who would be endangered if a rival son were to take the throne, David rouses himself and acts. Solomon is crowned. Bathsheba is safe.

What has happened between these two during the long years of their marriage?

The Bible is silent, but there are many clues. We know, for instance, that the relationship which had begun with betrayal was transformed into loyalty. David had confessed his sin. Bathsheba forgave him. What began as mere passion deepened into love. More than bodies joined to create their four sons: hearts entwined, too.

It was not passion that moved David to promise Bathsheba that their fourth son, Solomon, would succeed him as king. It was not passion that moved David to use his last strength to protect Bathsheba. It was not passion that moved a man like David to a commitment that we know lasted over many years.

And of course, by that final scene, when Bathsheba knelt beside the aged and dying king, she was no longer "desirable." But then, to hold David's love and affection for that long, Bathsheba must surely have been more than just another pretty face. Jewish rabbis maintain an ancient tradition which says Proverbs 31:10–31, which celebrates and honors the wife of noble character, was written by Solomon in honor of his mother, Bathsheba. If this is true, perhaps we can better understand why David learned to treasure and not just desire her.

Perhaps, too, the passage in Proverbs gives us some insight into the character of this betrayed woman who found the strength and courage not only to forgive, but to build a solid marriage on the ashes of her pain.

Bathsheba.

Bathsheba, patron saint of the betrayed.

Bathsheba, the woman who understands what it means for a man you trust to let you down.

And who understands even more.

M'Liss understands that "even more," too. After years of abuse, M'Liss finally went to the police. She filed a complaint under Minnesota's new domestic abuse law. When Chuck found out, he shouted and raved at her. But M'Liss remained firm. She wanted help—for her, and for him.

The day of the court hearing came.

"How do you plead?" Chuck was asked.

"Guilty."

And that was the beginning of a new life for both M'Liss and Chuck.

In group therapy each began to understand something of what had happened in their relationship. They found that their situation wasn't unique—that there are thousands just like them.

Chuck learned to understand his angry outbursts. M'Liss learned to recognize the signs of stress that often led up to them. Each of them learned how to communicate better in their marriage.

Today, five years later, M'Liss reports that "there hasn't been any violence in our marriage."

That doesn't mean that M'Liss and Chuck are home free. They continue to work at their relationship. And they serve as volunteers, working with other couples whose marriages have been marked by violence.

Like Bathsheba, M'Liss knows what it means to have

the person you trust most in life let you down. And like
Bathsheba, M'Liss knows that even betrayal need not be
the end.

So what about Kerri?
What about that letter in which she asked me, "Am I
bound to seek reconciliation with this man?"
And what about you?
Does God promise that if you just try harder when
you're abused and betrayed by someone to whom
you've entrusted your whole life, everything will all
work out fine?
No, not at all.
What we have in the story of Bathsheba and David,
reflected in the experience of M'Liss and Chuck, is
simply an indication that betrayal does not *have to be*
the end.
What does it take to transform such tragic failures
into marital success? Here are three guidelines:

(1) *There must be confession.* David accepted responsibility for his sinful acts. He confessed them to
God—and publicly. If David had been unwilling to ac-
knowledge his faults, there would have been no hope for
redemption in this relationship.
This was true for Chuck and M'Liss, too. The change
in their relationship came when M'Liss finally determined to force Chuck to accept responsibility for his
actions—and when Chuck chose to plead guilty.
No relationship will improve if a person who constantly betrays our trust refuses to accept his or her
responsibility and to confess the fault. As long as that
person continues to say, "You made me angry," or "You
did that to upset me," in effect blaming "you" for his or

her actions, there is practically no hope for change.

If you have been abused or betrayed in other ways by your spouse or any other person, don't expect the situation to improve until that person is willing to confess that *he* or *she* sinned.

(2) *There must be forgiveness.* With confession, there can be forgiveness. And forgiveness heals.

Like confession, Christian forgiveness is a way of dealing with reality. Forgiveness doesn't mean pretending the other person hasn't hurt us. It doesn't mean pretending that everything's all right. Christian forgiveness, like God's own forgiveness, looks honestly at the situation and says, "You have done wrong."

But then forgiveness affirms, "I love you and value you anyway. And I won't hold what you have done against you."

It's hard to forgive when, like Bathsheba or M'Liss, you have been violated. Used. Betrayed. I can't even urge you to forgive if something like this has happened to you. Forgiveness is a product of God's grace—you must ask him for the strength to extend forgiveness.

But Jesus once told a story about a man who owed his king millions of dollars and couldn't pay. He begged the ruler for more time. But the king, moved with compassion for him, actually canceled the debt! Jesus went on to describe how that same man angrily confronted a fellow citizen who owed him just a few dollars, insisting every penny be paid.

The point of the story was so clear. People who have been forgiven an unpayable debt are to be willing to forgive the lesser debts others owe them.

It helps me, when I find it hard to forgive someone, to remember that. The hurt the other person has caused me simply cannot compare with the debt I owe God.

God has forgiven me so much.

Considering Jesus, I can find the grace to forgive the person who owes me.

(3) *There must be rededication.* Rededication means more than saying, "OK, I'll try." It means commitment.

Rededication is a conscious decision to care. It is a willingness to work at rebuilding a shattered relationship. It means recognizing that it may be years before the hurt is totally healed and trust completely restored.

Where these three realities exist—confession, forgiveness, and rededication—there is hope.

The hurt, even of betrayal, can be healed.

And even violated trust can be restored.

For Meditation or Discussion

1. Look back at the sections of Kerri's letter quoted in chapter 1. Do you think a trust relationship between her and her husband can be restored? Why or why not? If you were in Kerri's situation, what do you think would be the best thing to do?

2. Bathsheba is one of the Bible's unsung heroines. She was far more than a sex object, although David used her as one in the beginning. Her forgiveness of David and the relationship she built with him reveal her to have been a quality person indeed. Review the story in 1 Kings 1, and look at Proverbs 31:10–31. What qualities of Bathsheba might serve as a model for a woman presently in a difficult domestic situation?

3. If you are an abused spouse or have a friend who is abused, you might consider a toll-free hotline operated by the National Coalition Against Domestic Violence. The line is open twenty-four hours a day, seven days a week, and someone there will be willing to talk about your situation and tell you about services available in your area. The number is 1-800-333-SAFE.

5

Shrewd as
Snakes

The procedure was more painful than Sue expected. Even with the local anesthetic, the three injections that were forced into her back around the ruptured disk hurt—really hurt.

That night and the next day Sue's back was worse than ever. Then she began to experience other pains. Her stomach ached. She had hot flashes and woke up during the night wringing wet with sweat. Her left leg grew so numb that she could hardly put in the clutch when she had to shift gears driving to work. Several times each day, her blood pressure dropped, and she felt totally exhausted. When Sue felt sudden sharp pains in her chest, shooting up into her right shoulder and down her arm, she became frightened. What was happening?

Finally Sue went to a local pharmacy to look up in their resource books the side effects of the cortisone they'd injected into her spine. Every one of the symptoms she was experiencing was listed there! And no one had warned her what to expect.

The doctor had acted as if it was nothing.

Just a couple of shots.

He hadn't even told her she might feel bad for a few days and should arrange to take off work.

And the anesthetist—when Sue had been frightened there at the hospital, he had self-righteously insisted, "We take away pain. We don't give it."

Now that it was too late, Sue felt so foolish. She should have found out everything before she let them work on her. She should never have trusted those doctors.

That's the way Jim and Karen felt after being swindled out of their savings by Carl Bowen. They had been impressed by that Mercedes limousine, the big house, the fine dinner, and the cruise on Carl's yacht. It never crossed their minds that Carl might not be just what he appeared: a very wealthy man who was willing to help them get rich, too.

Actually, Jim and Karen had more reason to trust Carl than do many people who fall for swindles. Every year, thousands of people send off their savings to purchase unseen gold or diamonds urgently peddled by some fast-talking stranger who telephones them, promises fantastic returns, and says that they have to act *now* or miss the chance of a lifetime.

Every day, people believe other callers who congratulate them for winning a trip—and then ask for a bank card number, "just to confirm you're the right John Smith." People give the credit card information. And later they are amazed to find charges on their monthly statement for merchandise they never purchased.

Oh, the swindles are endless.

A stranger comes to your door and offers to seal the cracks in your driveway. It just happens that his company had a job in your area that didn't take as much sealer as expected, and there's just enough left to do your drive. Of course, you'd be doing them a favor to finish off the truckload, so you can have the job done for less than half the regular price! You jump at the bargain.

Then the first rain washes away the "sealer," which was actually just a thin film of used oil.

Or another stranger in an official-looking uniform comes to your door. He's a furnace inspector, and he needs to look at your heating system to make sure there's no danger of fire. You let him into your basement, and he not only looks at your furnace—he takes it half apart. Then he comes up and tells you the bad news. An expensive part has to be replaced, or your furnace will surely explode sometime that winter. He knows someone who'll do a good job for you. If you don't buy, the "inspector" just walks away, leaving your furnace disassembled on the basement floor.

Even guarantees are no guarantee. The ad offers real silver coins, sure to increase in value. For a limited time, you can get them for only twenty-five dollars a coin. And if you're not fully satisfied, you can return the coins within thirty days and all your money will be cheerfully refunded. Oh yes, there's a limit on the number of coins you can purchase. Others will want to take advantage of this special opportunity too.

The ad pictures coins in mint condition. But when yours finally arrive, you're shocked to see the coins are so worn that they are worthless as collector's items. You send for your money back, only to get a mimeographed note saying, "Sorry, the money cannot be refunded because you did not fulfill the necessary conditions."

What happened?

Why, when your order was received it was filled immediately, and the package with your coins was run through a dated postage meter. Then your package was left sitting in the seller's office, to be mailed only when the "thirty days" would pass before you even got your coins. By the time you opened the package, your "guarantee" had already expired.

Jesus sums it up in an observation found in one of his parables: "The people of this world are more shrewd in dealing with their own kind than are the people of light" (Luke 16:8).

Maybe we'd put it this way:

It's dumb to trust strangers.

There are just too many people out there trying to take you.

Somehow, we don't want to believe that. When much of Stephen Breuning's medical research at the University of Pittsburgh was exposed as fraudulent, the editor of *Science* wrote in an editorial, "we must recognize that 99.9999 percent of reports are accurate and truthful."

Somehow his claim that there is only one bad apple in every million seems naïve in view of recent events. Look at the record of the medical profession alone. According to the 8 June 1987, issue of *U.S. News and World Report,*

- Dr. Robert Slutsky resigned from the School of Medicine at the University of California, San Diego, after committing "extensive research fraud" over a six-year period.
- A research team at Harvard's Dana-Farber Cancer Institute formally reported a major discovery, later to find that a graduate student had faked key results of an experiment.
- Three papers published in the *Journal of the American Chemical Society* were retracted when the validity of their research was challenged.
- Cornell University Medical College repeatedly denied an "error" in a published paper by one of its leading faculty members, until forced to admit it.

Five years later, other charges against the same faculty member still have not been resolved.[1]

One bad apple in a million? Hardly.

Are most people in business trustworthy? Well, 1987 was the year of Ivan Boeskey, whose hundreds of millions of profits were gained by insider trading. All this means is that Boeskey and others accused with him made their money by using information not available to the general public. They profited by buying or selling stocks *at the expense of other investors*. Every dollar they made, someone else lost. And those accused in the scandal include the top corporate officers of some of America's most respected brokerage firms.

No, it's not just the fast-talking telephone salesman in some boiler-room operation who is out to take you. It may be the broker who advises you to sell, not because selling is to your advantage, but so he can generate extra commissions. Or it might be the mechanic who says you need a new carburetor, when maybe all he has to do is reattach a wire that's come loose (or that he loosened last time you brought your car in for an oil change).

What it boils down to is that we really do live in a world warped by sin, a world peopled with sinful persons.

It's nice to be trusting—but it isn't always smart.

Before this all becomes too much of a downer, let's note something important. The people we've been looking at in this chapter are *distant*.

They're not people you know well.

They're not people who know you well.

They're more or less strangers.

1. Daniel Greenberg, "Publish or perish—or fake it," *U.S. News & World Report*, 8 June 1987, pp.72–73.

And the trust you have in strangers with whom you do business is very different from the trust you develop in a parent, a spouse, or in a close friend.

When you do trust a stranger and he or she lets you down, you don't really feel hurt. You feel shame.

Instead of thinking, "How could he do that to me?" you think, "How could I have been such a fool?"

Down deep, we all know that the people of this world are all too likely to put profit before people, cash before concern.

Since we live in a world like this, it makes sense not to be too trusting of strangers.

This doesn't mean that we have to be paranoid, peering suspiciously at every unfamiliar face while clutching our wallets close to our hearts. It simply means that being Christian doesn't necessarily mean being naïve. Jesus put it like this in a charge to his disciples: "I am sending you out like sheep among wolves. Therefore be as shrewd as snakes and as innocent as doves. Be on your guard against men" (Matt. 10:16–17).

How can we be on guard against the human wolves that rove our world? And what might being "shrewd as snakes" involve? Here are nine helpful guidelines from the Book of Proverbs:

(1) *"Guard your heart" (Prov. 4:23).* Typically, strangers who hope to take advantage of trusting individuals rely on a common motive. They appeal to the desire to make money, and they promise fantastic returns on investments. Proverbs comments dryly, "He who chases fantasies lacks judgment" (12:11). And Paul writes in 1 Timothy 6:9, "People who want to get rich fall into temptation and a trap."

We can protect ourselves against the wolves of society by first checking our own motives. We should be suspicious of anything that makes our heart beat faster at the thought of large, quick, and easy profits.

(2) *"Every prudent man acts out of knowledge"* *(Prov. 13:16).* Whether we're thinking of an investment, considering some medical procedure, or just planning to buy a VCR, this principle is important. We need to learn everything we can before we act.

Sue's doctor told her she needed cortisone injections in her back. She trusted him, and she didn't find out ahead of time about the possible side effects or alternate procedures. What she should have done was listen, then come back later with a list of questions about the procedure. She should have gone to the pharmacy *before* the procedure and checked out side effects in the resource books every pharmacy has.

It's the same with any significant decision we have to make. There are books and magazines we can study before investing. There are magazines that rate VCRs.

Before we act on *anyone's* advice, remember, "Every prudent man acts out of knowledge."

(3) *"Make plans by seeking advice"* *(Prov. 20:18).* It's not enough to listen to one doctor or one fast-talking salesman who urges you to act quickly before the opportunity is gone. Seek advice before you act. Go to another doctor and get a second opinion. Call up the Better Business Bureau while that truck with the cement sealer waits in your driveway.

It's always unwise to act on the urging of just one individual. As Proverbs observes, "The first to present his case seems right, till another comes forward and questions him" (18:17).

(4) *"A prudent man gives thought to his steps" (Prov. 14:15).* Whenever anyone presses you for a quick decision, be warned. That "opportunity" you'll miss if you don't send in your money *right away* is almost certainly an opportunity you should avoid!

Take time to think about your next step before making any commitment. And while you're waiting, go back to principle 2 and use the time to learn more about the action you're being urged to take.

(5) *"Many a man claims to have unfailing love" (Prov. 20:16).* Another warning flag is raised when a stranger claims that he's doing something for you because he "just plain loves you." Maybe. But I can't help wondering about the auto dealership that advertises low prices on our local cable TV, insisting that they don't care about profits but just want to give their customers a good deal.

Jesus said that even the wicked of this world know how to give good gifts—to their children. He didn't suggest that they're eager to give things away to strangers.

In fact, Proverbs 12:26 says that "a righteous man is cautious in friendship." The stranger who is eager to give you a special deal just because he loves you so much is more likely the subject of another Proverb: "A lying tongue hates those it hurts" (26:28).

(6) *"The prudent see danger and take refuge, but the simple keep on going and suffer for it" (Prov. 27:12).* One of the favorite ploys of the telephone salesman is to get a small initial investment and then to keep coming back for more. Once you've been sucked in, it's hard to say no, even if you've become suspicious.

It may be the same with your doctor. It surely should have been this way with that editor of *Science* who, after publishing fraudulent research reports, still insisted that only one person in a million would do such a thing.

Because they are embarrassed by their gullibility, people often reject their suspicions and tell themselves that nothing could possibly be wrong. But when a prudent man even glimpses danger, he knows it's time to take refuge.

You can keep going if you want. But most likely you'll suffer for it.

(7) *"Press your plea with your neighbor"* *(Prov. 6:3).* If you have been harmed by a stranger who has violated your trust, don't just let it go. Talk to the person first. If you get no satisfaction, take other steps.

If the problem is with a doctor, write a factual report of what happened and send it to the local medical association. They have a committee that studies the merits of such complaints and can discipline their members. If serious harm has been done, see a lawyer.

If you've been the victim of fraud, call the appropriate law enforcement agency and, again, see a lawyer. Or call your local newspaper or TV station; many have a special column or show that takes up the cause of those who have a complaint against area businesses.

You may not recover what you've lost. But your action might keep someone else from becoming a victim, too.

(8) *"Do not say, . . . 'I'll pay that man back for what he did'"* *(Prov. 24:29).* You can take responsible action to recover your losses and protect others without being vengeful. Watch out for the anger that often comes with the feeling of having been fooled.

Paul says in Romans 12:19, "Do not take revenge, my friends, but leave room for God's wrath, for it is written: 'It is mine to avenge; I will repay,' says the Lord."

How good to know that ultimately the really foolish person is the man who takes advantage of others for momentary gain, never realizing that one day he must face the judgment of God!

(9) *"Commit to the Lord whatever you do" (Prov. 16:3).* This guideline is a companion to each of the others. We need always to take advantage of God's promise to be with us and guide us as we look to him. Prayer is a vital part of every Christian's decision-making process.

For Meditation and Discussion

1. Share with someone else a situation in which you either made or were pressured to make decisions urged by strangers. What did you do? Why? What was the outcome?

2. What are some situations in which we have to trust strangers? Which of the guidelines from Proverbs do you think is most important then? Which is hardest to follow? Which are you personally most likely to follow?

3. Imagine that you've moved to a new city and want to select a family doctor. Using the guidelines in this chapter, make a list of specific steps you might take to be sure you have the best doctor available.

6

My Hand Will
Not Touch You

Crouching far back in deep shadows, David and his men gazed tensely at the brightness marking the entrance of the cave. Outside, three thousand soldiers searched for them, urged on by the jealous King Saul.

Then a single figure momentarily blocked off the light—and stepped inside the cave.

It was the king himself, entering, as the Bible text delicately says, "to relieve himself."

David's men whispered urgently.

This was David's opportunity!

God had actually handed David's great enemy over to him! Look! The king was squatting now, face toward the cave entrance, his back to the dangerous men he hunted.

Now, David!

Now!

Stealthily David approached his enemy, blade in hand. Saul had never been more vulnerable.

David reached out—but rather than drive the knife into his enemy's back, he sliced off a piece of Saul's robe.

Then, just as stealthily, David slipped away into the deeper darkness at the back of the cave.

First Samuel 24 picks up the story after Saul has left the cave and moved on. In its telling of this incident, the

Bible teaches you and me much about trust—and trust-worthiness.

Then David went out of the cave and called out to Saul, "My lord the king!" When Saul looked behind him, David bowed down and prostrated himself with his face to the ground. He said to Saul, "Why do you listen when men say, 'David is bent on harming you'? This day you have seen with your own eyes how the Lord delivered you into my hands in the cave. Some urged me to kill you, but I spared you; I said, 'I will not lift my hand against my master, because he is the Lord's anointed.' See, my father, look at this piece of your robe in my hand! I cut off the corner of your robe but did not kill you. Now understand and recognize that I am not guilty of wrongdoing or rebellion. I have not wronged you, but you are hunting me down to take my life. May the Lord judge between you and me. And may the Lord avenge the wrongs you have done to me, but my hand will not touch you. As the old saying goes, 'From evildoers come evil deeds,' so my hand will not touch you. . . ."

When David finished saying this, Saul asked, "Is that your voice, David my son?" Then he wept aloud. "You are more righteous than I," he said. "You have treated me well, but I have treated you badly. You have just now told me of the good you did to me; the Lord delivered me into your hands, but you did not kill me. When a man finds his enemy, does he let him get away unharmed? May the Lord reward you well for the way you treated me today. I know that you will surely be king and that the kingdom of Israel will be established in your hands. Now swear to me by the Lord that you will not cut off my descendants or wipe out my name from my father's family."

So David gave his oath to Saul. Then Saul returned home, but David and his men went up to the stronghold (vv. 8–22).

It's strange how many enemies we seem to have. What's even stranger, many of our enemies are our closest friends.

What I mean is that people we care about, people whom we think care about us, are the ones who most often wound us.

Take the woman who wrote to Ann Landers, signing herself "Empty Cradle." She told about the reaction of her friends to her twelfth miscarriage. One said, "You must have miscounted." Another felt called to give advice: "Accept the fact that you weren't meant to have children, and get your tubes tied." Then there was the spiritual giant who said, "God is trying to tell you something. Listen to him." But it was a relative who tried to trivialize the woman's pain, saying, "Each miscarriage must be easier to handle."

Empty Cradle wrote,

> The truth is, each miscarriage is more difficult. Every time it happens, I lose faith all over again.
> In a store last week I saw a baby with the face I've dreamed of dozens of times. The young mother didn't push me away when I touched his little foot. Suddenly I started to cry. She held her baby with one arm and me with the other and asked, "Are you OK?" I was embarrassed and said, "I'm fine." Then I hurried out of the store.
> I want to say thank you to that woman who tried to make me feel better. I wonder, Ann, if a stranger can be so compassionate, why can't my friends and family understand?

Psychological wounds are not the only ones inflicted by loved ones. One study showed that many married persons with AIDS continue to have sex with their uninfected mates—without using condoms. According to *St. Petersburg Times* staff writer Carol Gentry, in spite of the fact that couples were repeatedly told the dangers of unprotected sex, they dismissed the warnings because condoms interfered with their fun! Reportedly, 20 percent of those interviewed just "don't like to use them." And a whopping 40 percent complained that condoms decreased sensation. The vow to love and cherish somehow seemed irrelevant compared to a little extra sensation, even when that extra sensation was obtained by threatening a loved one with a painful and always fatal disease.

As a result, in this study of forty-seven couples, of the thirty-five couples who continued having sex, seventeen of the healthy spouses became infected with the AIDS virus!

I know something like this is hard for us to believe. But actually, it's hard to imagine most of the wounds that we receive from people we trust.

It's hard for Empty Cradle to imagine how her friends and relatives can be so insensitive toward her pain.

It's also hard for Mario, whom I introduced in chapter 1, to believe that his parents have cut him out of their will. After all the loving care he's lavished on them for so long. After all those nights working without pay to make sure mom and dad's business wouldn't fail because they were too old to keep check on everything. Mario is sure that his sister, the one who's never there, manipulated mom and dad into cutting him off. It's hard not to let the hurt turn to anger.

It was hard for Ellen to believe that her best friend wouldn't speak to her. It's even harder to be-lieve that she gossips and laughs about the painful, personal things Ellen has shared with her in confidence.

And it must have been hard for David. Hard to believe that King Saul, who had honored him and urged him to marry his own daughter, now was absolutely determined to kill him.

The problem is, when we do finally believe that a person or persons we trust has let us down, how do we respond? How do we handle the hurt? How do we respond to the person who has been insensitive or acted hostilely toward us?

The answer we find in the Bible is simple yet profound. We make a commitment to God, to ourselves, and to the person who has violated our trust. That commitment is, "My hand will not touch you."

God doesn't ask us to ignore the hurt.

God doesn't ask us to pretend there's been no change in our feelings toward the person we once trusted.

God doesn't ask us to keep on being so vulnerable that we are hurt again and again.

God does ask us to make David's choice—to make a commitment like his.

However much we have been hurt, we will not strike back.

We will not take revenge.

"My hand will not touch you."

Several things in the Bible's report of this incident help us see the wisdom of David's difficult decision and show us why the course David took is the best one for you and me:

(1) *We establish a standard.* David himself would one day be king. He would need the loyalty of all around him. By honoring Saul as God's anointed and refusing to harm the king who was his enemy, David established a standard of loyalty for his followers.

You and I live in a world where people strike back at those who harm them, a world where the Golden Rule is cynically restated, "Do unto others, before they can do unto you!" We live with people—our children, our friends, our co-workers, our fellow church members— who need to experience, and not just know, standards of godly behavior. We live with people who need to have righteousness modeled for them.

David's determination not to strike out at Saul provided just such a model for his men. It established a standard of right behavior for his coming kingdom.

You and I are called, as Jesus' people, to set standards for the world.

We will reach few by ranting against their sins or pointing out their failures. But we can touch people deeply by our example and by the standard our behavior sets.

(2) *We find freedom.* David did not excuse Saul, who truly was to be blamed for his hostility toward David and for his sinful acts. What David did was to consciously bring God into the picture. We see this in his words: "May the Lord judge between you and me. And may the Lord avenge the wrongs you have done to me" (1 Sam. 24:12).

All too often, our reaction to hurt or hostility is to strike back. We see the issue as something between Mario and his sister or between Ellen and her gossipy one-time friend. We listen to the popular wisdom, which says "If you don't look out for yourself, no one else will," and we determine to get even. If she hurts me, I'll zap her right back! Then maybe she'll think twice before she does it again.

The other choice people sometimes make seems even worse. They give in to their hurt and simply crumble, making themselves victims and looking to others for pity. They are too weak to protect themselves.

And in advertising their weakness, such people invite more hurt.

Many of us feel trapped between these two responses when hurt by others. If we don't strike back, we will look—and feel—weak. So, rather than accepting the shame of feeling the victim, most of us tend to strike back.

David avoided both these relational pitfalls. He faced the fact of Saul's hostility and sinful acts. And he consciously committed his cause to God. God could punish Saul as the Lord wished. David would neither strike out at Saul nor be his victim.

In saying, "The Lord judge between you and me," David found a freedom that is available to us when we are hurt. By committing the issue to God, we release ourselves from the need to strike back. And we release ourselves from the need to feel weak and ashamed.

(3) *We soften hard hearts.* David's action had an effect even on Saul. True, it was a temporary effect, but it was powerful. The Bible says Saul wept aloud and even confessed, "You are more righteous than I. . . . You have treated me well, but I have treated you badly" (1 Sam. 24:17).

Saul then led his army home. Later, in the grip of paranoid fears, Saul would once again pursue David. But for the moment, David's action had softened Saul's heart. For the moment, Saul's soul was open to glimpse God's redeeming grace.

This is a ministry we Christians are called to have toward people who act like enemies. Paul says, "Do not repay anyone evil for evil" (Rom. 12:17), and goes on to quote from Proverbs: "If your enemy is hungry, feed him; if he is thirsty, give him something to drink." Our calling as Jesus' people is to "not be overcome by evil, but overcome evil with good" (vv. 20–21). What a fascinating thought!

The person who does us harm feels that he has won a victory. But he or she has won a victory only if the hurt leads us to sin in return! We have the most powerful spiritual weapon that exists—good. When we return good for evil, we can overcome evil.

We may even open to the grace of God the heart of the person who hurts us. Perhaps just for a moment. Perhaps . . . for eternity.

(4) *We establish God's kingdom.* The most poignant words in this Old Testament story were uttered by Saul. Just before returning home, Saul cried out, "I know that you will surely be king and that the kingdom of Israel will be established in your hands. Now swear to me by the Lord that you will not cut off my descendants or wipe out my name from my father's family" (1 Sam. 24:20–21).

He was referring to an old established pagan custom. Whenever a new dynasty had been established in pagan lands, the new king had killed all the members of the preceding ruler's family. This guaranteed that no one would mount a rebellion by raising up a member of the previous royal family and appealing to the people's old loyalties. Later, that pagan practice had been followed by many rulers in the northern half of Saul's divided kingdom.

Now Saul, acknowledging David's destiny, begged that this man he had tried so hard to murder would protect Saul's descendants!

Once David had trusted Saul—his king, his commander, and his father-in-law. Saul had proven unworthy of David's trust. But somehow the king knew that, despite what he had done to David, David could be trusted with the lives of Saul's descendants. The kingdom would be established in David's hands. And David would never violate Saul's trust.

One day Jesus will return, and the entire earth will become the kingdom of God. Even now, wherever Jesus rules—in your heart or in mine—the kingdom is here. How wonderful to know that, as we make the commitment David made, God's kingdom can be established in our lives!

And even those who hurt us will know it!

Even those we cannot trust will realize that they can trust us.

There's no guarantee that making David's commitment will insulate us from being hurt. Determining "my hand will not touch you" simply does not insure that people we trust will never let us down nor be insensitive.

But it does lessen the chances!

Luke's Gospel reports a fascinating saying uttered by Jesus just after he called on his followers to love their enemies. According to Luke 6:37–38, Jesus said,

> Do not judge, and you will not be judged. Do not condemn, and you will not be condemned. Forgive, and you will be forgiven. Give, and it will be given to you. A good measure, pressed down, shaken together and running over, will be poured into your lap. For with the measure you use, it will be measured to you.

Some have taken this as a promise that God will bless us for doing right. And of course, that sentiment is true— but that's not what Jesus is saying here.

Jesus is talking about the "norm of reciprocity"—the fact that others tend to treat us as we treat them. If we invite friends over for dinner, they can probably be expected to invite us, also. If we do someone a favor, we can probably expect them to do us a favor. And, of course, if we do harm to someone, the norm of reciprocity expresses the fact that they will probably try to do harm to us.

The measure you use is the measure others probably will use in relating to you.

What Jesus is saying in this context is absolutely exciting. *Jesus' call to love our enemies is a call to establish a new relationship with them—a relationship in which they can be changed by the power of love!*

If you strike back when someone strikes you, the cycle of hostility and violence is simply reinforced. When you determine, "my hand will not touch you," you break the cycle. And not only that—you may even establish a new and different cycle!

If you refuse to judge others, others may stop judging you.

If you refuse to condemn, others may stop condemning you.

If you forgive, others may learn to forgive you.

If you give, others may give to you.

By your decision, "my hand will not touch you," you may teach others not only to trust you—but to become trustworthy themselves.

For Meditation and Discussion

1. The first step in finding strength to respond to hurts as David did is to consciously commit our cause to the Lord. What is there in your relationships with others that you need to commit to God for judgment right now?

2. Read the story in 1 Samuel 24 several times. Let God highlight verses and phrases that he wants you to take to heart. What do you believe is the most important teaching of this chapter for you personally?

3. Share with others some experiences in which you have been hurt by the insensitivity or actual hostility of people close to you. How did you react? How did you feel? How might these insights from David's life affect your feelings and responses should you be hurt again in the future?

7

Success
Story

Peter settled back in his easy chair.

It was good to be home again, even for just a few days' break from traveling.

Peter always felt a surge of something when he entered his house in Capernaum. Some might call it pride. Peter called it contentment.

What was it that reporter from the *Jerusalem Post* had called his home? Oh yes. A "solid symbol of hard-earned success."

That was true, of course. No false modesty for Peter. After all, everything Peter had accomplished reflected glory on God. Peter had been careful to express this to the reporter. He'd even quoted from Deuteronomy, just as the Master did when he was tempted. "Remember the Lord your God," Peter had repeated, "for it is he who gives you the ability to produce wealth" (8:18).

For the ten-thousandth time, Peter closed his eyes and thanked God. He thanked God for all his blessings, and especially for the way the Lord had blessed him with success after success.

Peter didn't look like a religious person. He was of more than average height, with powerful shoulders and hands. His face was deeply lined, its tough, wind-

battered skin the color of dark olive wood. His hair and
beard were more white now than dark, yet no one would
have thought him old. In fact, the dark eyes peering
from under heavy brows conveyed a sense of unusual
vitality. And in addition to being physically imposing,
Peter had the kind of dynamic and positive personality
that made him the leader in almost every activity.

Even now, Peter was the leader among the disciples
of Jesus. Whenever an article in the *Jerusalem Post*
listed Christ's disciples, Peter was named first—and
Peter was quoted more often than any of them. Later,
when Matthew and Mark and Luke would produce his-
tories of the time Peter was now living, the same thing
would happen. Peter would be first on every list, and
Peter would be quoted more often than the rest put
together.

A rugged, powerful man.

A successful man.

The one man everyone living along the shore of
Galilee would point to if a stranger asked, as many had,
for "the fisherman."

Peter's first success had come in the business world.
The Sea of Galilee provided fish for tables throughout
the Jewish homeland. The first-century historian Jose-
phus tells us that some three hundred thirty fishing
boats then worked that small body of water.

Peter was born in Bethsaida, a tiny fishing village
whose name appropriately meant "house of fish." With
his brother, Andrew, Peter had been taught the trade by
their father.

Fishing was hard work. Most fishing was done at night,
with a lighted torch attached to the bow of a heavy
wooden boat. The fishermen used both circular cast nets
with heavily weighted edges and long, even weightier

dragnets. It took two boats to use the dragnet—to position it and close the circle, then haul in the nets hand over hand.

But fishing took more than work—it took skill. Skill in knowing just where and when to put out the nets. Skill when a night's work was done to mend any tears. Skill to clean and preserve the catch by salting, smoking, or drying. And it took good business sense to set up a distribution network, arranging for the transportation and sale of the catch so the fisherman, not the middle man, received the profit from all that hard work. Peter had seen this clearly, and so he had gone into partnership with the sons of Zebedee. Together they had expanded their marketing into Jerusalem itself, where John, who handled that end of the business, was known even to the high priest himself!

It was a measure of Peter's success as a fisherman and a businessman that after a few years he had been able to move from Bethsaida to Capernaum and to purchase a large house there. As the reporter put it, that house in Capernaum was the solid symbol of Peter's hard-earned success.

Capernaum was the capital of the district. The governor was there, as was the tax office charged with collecting tolls on the trade route that ran along the lake. There was even a retired Roman centurion and some other army veterans who had decided to make the pleasant lake district their home.

Yet Capernaum, for all its significance, was squeezed between the lake and the high black hills that rose just beyond it. There was very little land available on that strip, and what there was was expensive. The move to Capernaum and the purchase of his house had cost Peter more than he liked to remember!

But it had been a wise move to get closer to the

district's business center. And, since the best fishing grounds on the sea then, as now, lay at the north end of Galilee, between Capernaum and Bethsaida, the move made no difference in the size of the partners' catch.

Besides, Peter *liked* living in one of the city's largest houses. Peter enjoyed his success and, like any pious Jew of his day, Peter was glad to ascribe that success to God—Blessed be he!

Relaxed, Peter let his mind rove on to his first meetings with Jesus.

Andrew had run off to listen to John the Baptist, much to Peter's initial disgust. But after a couple of weeks, Peter too had pulled his boats ashore and traveled along the Jordan River to the place where John was preaching. He had arrived just after John's cousin from Galilee had been baptized and John had identified him as the Son of God. Andrew had introduced his brother to that cousin, and Peter had immediately been taken with the quiet, self-possessed stranger. Peter had always thought himself a good judge of men, and this man Jesus was something special.

Peter and Andrew and some of their friends had stayed with Jesus for a few days, and then Jesus had come down to Capernaum to visit them. He'd stayed at Peter's house, listening with interest as Peter showed him around and explained the fishing business. Then he'd gone back home to Nazareth, just a dozen miles or so from Capernaum itself. Peter had really liked Jesus. But even more, Peter had been impressed—particularly when they'd stopped off at Cana and Jesus had actually turned water into wine.

A few months later, Jesus had appeared along the seashore, followed by a crowd, and asked Peter to let him teach from one of his boats. Afterward, Jesus had told Peter to go on out in the boat and try fishing again.

Peter had felt a flash of resentment then. He knew fish, and there wouldn't be any fish along the shore that time of day. But because it was Jesus, and there really was something special about the man, Peter had done it—and suddenly the nets had been filled.

Well, it had been too much.

Peter had knelt on the shore and said, "Leave me alone, Lord, for I'm a sinful man." With Jesus, and only with Jesus, Peter had a terrible sense of his own inadequacies. But when Jesus had called him and all of his partners to follow him and be disciples, Peter had gotten right up and followed.

Peter wasn't a man to avoid a challenge.

He had the courage it took to make a midlife change of career.

Well, Peter was a success as a disciple, just as he'd been a success in the fishing business. He was the acknowledged leader of Jesus' Twelve. He was the first to ask questions of Jesus—and the first to answer the questions Jesus himself asked. Peter was the one who, with James and John, had special moments alone with the Master. Peter was the one Jesus had complimented, saying "Blessed are you, Simon son of Jonah." Peter was the one Jesus had called a "Rock," and to whom Jesus gave the "keys of the kingdom of heaven."

Of course, Jesus also had rebuked Peter at times— such as the time Jesus was saying something about dying soon. Then Peter, as the senior disciple, had taken Jesus apart to advise him. "Never, Lord!" Peter had objected.

Well, that was the one time Jesus had really been angry with Peter. And the fisherman had realized even then that he had gone too far. After all, you can't call Jesus "the Christ, the Son of the living God" in one breath and in the next breath tell God what to do!

Peter would never make *that* mistake again. Jesus was Lord, so Peter would let him *be* Lord.

It was enough for Peter to be a disciple. A successful disciple.

With that comforting thought, Peter relaxed even more, and drifted off to sleep.

The incident I've just portrayed is imaginary, of course. There was no *Jerusalem Post* in the first century—and no easy chairs. But the details of Peter's life are accurate, reconstructed not only from the Gospels but from archaeology.

Peter was a success.

He was a success in business. He was a success as a disciple. Later, Peter would be an even greater success as a leader of Christ's church.

In fact, Peter is the kind of person that the successful of every age can identify with. A go-getter. Hard driving. Intelligent. Aware. Willing to take risks. A motivator. Respected. A true leader of men.

That's why what happened to Peter next shook him so. The one person he had come to trust most let him down.

Jesus and his friends had shared their last supper together. It was late, but Jesus wanted to spend a few moments alone with God in a hillside garden across from Jerusalem. On the way there, Jesus told them, "this very night you will all fall away on account of me."

Peter was the first to reply, expressing the thought in all their minds: "Even if all fall away on account of you, I never will!"

Jesus then predicted Peter's denial. But still Peter wouldn't listen: "Even if I have to die with you, I will never disown you!"

Made bold by Peter's confidence, "all the other disciples said the same."

You know the rest of the story. When Jesus was taken by the mob, the disciples fled. But Peter followed the mob "at a distance" to see what they did with his Lord. Peter crept into the courtyard of the high priest while Jesus was being questioned inside. There a servant woman confronted him, charging Peter with being one of Jesus' followers—and Peter denied it. When others joined in the accusations, Peter, frightened, cursed and swore. "I don't even know the man!"

Then the cock crowed, and Peter remembered what Jesus had said: "Before the cock crows you will deny me three times." And Peter, broken, staggered outside where he "wept bitterly."

Peter had trusted—himself. And the person he trusted most had let him down!

The hymn that tops my list of "least favorites" is one that I suffer through in church at least once or twice a year. It bothers me, because apparently the hymn writer never grasped the lesson that Peter learned that dreadful night when he betrayed our Lord. Here are its familiar words:

> "Are ye able," said the Master,
> "To be crucified with me?"
> "Yea," the sturdy dreamers answered,
> "To the death we follow Thee."
>
> "Lord, we are able,"
> Our spirits are Thine.
> Remold them, make us
> Like Thee, divine:
> Thy guiding radiance
> Above us shall be
> A beacon to God,
> To love and loyalty.

The hymn concludes,

> "Are ye able?" still the Master
> Whispers down eternity,
> And heroic spirits answer
> Now, as then in Galilee.

> "Lord, we are able,"
> our spirits are Thine. . . . °

Well, our spirits *are* God's. And as Jesus said, the spirit is willing. But as Jesus also said, the flesh is weak. Trust in any human being—even in ourselves—is ill advised, especially if in our trusting we assume we'll never let ourselves down.

There's an important point here.

Yes, we do—and we *should*—trust others and ourselves. But we dare not assume that the person we trust will never let us down.

Every human being ever born, with just one exception, was a born sinner. Every person, with one exception, has flaws. Every person but one can, and at some time almost surely will, let us down.

Peter, the successful first-century man, failed to realize that he too might fail. His accomplishments in business, in personal relationships, and in discipleship made him blind to his own vulnerability. He had never really heard or taken into account the words of Isaiah 2:22: "Stop trusting in man, who has but a breath in his nostrils. Of what account is he?"

When Peter finally did let himself down, he was crushed; he wept bitterly. Even after Christ had risen from the dead, Peter had difficulty coping with his failure. John's Gospel tells us that after Jesus had shown

---

° Earl Marlatt, 1925.

himself alive to his disciples, Peter said, "I'm going fishing." His spiritual failure had so discouraged Peter that he turned back to the one thing at which he knew he could succeed—fishing.

All too often, we're like Peter.

We succeed in so many ways. Then, when we fail spiritually, we're crushed. We can't believe that we, of all people, would fail so miserably. We're ashamed, and we're uncertain of how our failure has affected our relationship with God. How can we have any value to God after having done something so terrible? How can we make any contribution to Jesus' kingdom now?

If you've ever felt like this, the story of Peter holds three important lessons for you:

(1) *"Stop trusting in man."* These words of Isaiah have echoed for nearly three thousand years, testifying to the fact that each of us is vulnerable to failure.

So listen to what God has said through his prophet. You or I may have as many accomplishments. We may be as respected as Peter was and may even have progressed to spiritual leadership. But we too are vulnerable.

Paul wrote to the Corinthians, "If you think you are standing firm, be careful that you don't fall" (1 Cor. 10:12). We are most likely to stumble just when we think that we are most successful!

(2) *Do trust in Jesus.* Jesus is never surprised nor shocked with the failure of successful Christians. He knows the full extent of our weakness. And he loves us anyway.

Look at Jesus' love for Peter.

The morning Peter went back to fishing, Jesus appeared on the shore. He cooked breakfast and then asked Peter, "Do you love me?" Peter professed the love he felt, the love he had never lost despite his failure.

And Jesus said, "Take care of my sheep."

Peter had worried that his failure might destroy his relationship with the Lord. It didn't. Jesus looked for Peter and found him. Jesus led Peter to see that failure did not mean that Peter had lost his love for Jesus; it simply meant that Peter had relied too much on himself and not enough on God.

And then Jesus recommissioned Peter, challenging him as his disciple to care for Christ's other sheep.

When you fail, Jesus seeks you out, too. He reminds you that despite your weaknesses you do love him. And Jesus, knowing your weaknesses far better than you do, trusts those he loves into your care.

(3) *Commit yourself to discipleship.* Peter accepted the commission given him to care for Jesus' sheep. The Book of Acts tells of Peter's new boldness—and of the great response to Peter's preaching.

It was into the hands of a failed disciple that Jesus committed the founding of his Church.

And this time Peter *didn't* fail.

This is an important lesson for us. Our failures do not mark an end of our usefulness to God.

In fact, failure may be the key to usefulness. Only the person who has learned not to trust himself, who relies wholly on the Lord, will be spiritually productive.

Trusting Jesus fully, and recommitted to his discipleship, Peter truly did succeed.

And so can you.

Whatever your failures.

However you have let down God—and yourself.

Jesus still seeks you, and when he finds you again you'll learn that your failure was simply a necessary prelude to your spiritual success.

For Meditation and Discussion

1. Jot down a few words that describe how Peter must have felt after denying Jesus. Using these feelings as a guide, locate times when you feel you, too, let down God and/or yourself.

2. How is the following summary statement from this chapter supported by the Bible's account (read John 18:15–27; John 21; Acts 4, 11)?:

   Only the person who has learned not to trust himself, who relies wholly on the Lord, will be spiritually productive.

3. Consider this famous theological formulation: In Christ it is not impossible for us to sin, but it is possible for us not to sin. No matter how we have let ourselves down spiritually, the possibility of a victorious life in Christ is open to us as we trust fully in the Lord.

8

Puppy
Love

Janet Geringer Woititz starts one of her little books by saying, "A child is very much like a puppy . . . offering and receiving love freely and easily, scampering, somewhat mischievous, playful, doing work for approval or reward, but doing as little as possible. Most important, being *carefree*."

And then she adds, "If a child is like a puppy, you were not a child."

The quote is from one of Woititz's little bestsellers, a booklet called *Adult Children of Alcoholics.** Woititz, who is president of the Institute for Counseling and Training, Verona, New Jersey, and a nationally known speaker, specializes in helping adults who had alcoholic parents. Her booklet summarizes the impact of one of life's greatest and most common tragedies and answers a question no one wants to ask:

What happens when the people you *have* to trust—your parents—let you down?

We all tend to idealize the family. We should. Home, you see, really is a place for puppy love. It's a place for

---

* (Pompano Beach, FL: Health Communications, 1983), p. 1.

115

hugs and cuddles. It's a place for warm nighttime kisses, for snuggling down into the blankets as mom or dad sits beside us to listen to our "Now I lay me down to sleep." Home is a place for repeated "Nos," for "Eat all your carrots," for "Carry me, Daddy." It's for taking a walk at night and running ahead while mom and dad hold hands and smile. Home is a place for puppy love. For scampering. For sly mischief. For play. For being carefree and safe.

The tragedy is that many of us never knew this kind of home. For many, home was a place for blows and curses. It was a place for cowering at night under the blankets as daddy beat mommy; where nighttime prayers were just "God, make them stop." Home was a place you were ashamed to bring your friends, a place you never knew what you'd find when you opened the door. Oh, there were times your dad was loving. Times when mom listened, laughed with you, cared. But other times he or she was drunk or out of control—and not loving at all.

And you never knew.

You could never be sure.

All the *carefree* spirit that marks normal childhood was gone. And with it you lost, not love for your parents, but something perhaps even more precious: trust.

You simply couldn't trust them.

You knew they were sure to let you down.

A dear friend of mine in Phoenix understands that feeling, although her dad wasn't a drunk. She's in her sixties now.

When she was a young girl, her mom grew sick. Her dad, a railroad worker, was morose and bitter. Then he began to slip into her room at night. At first he just caressed her, and she was so glad for this attention from her dad. Then one night he went further.

As she lay there, listening to the labored breathing of her mom in the next room, her dad got on top of her. She was so young. She didn't really know what was happening.

It didn't happen every night. She'd lie there, tense and frightened, waiting to see. All too often, when dad was in a dark mood, he would come.

She could see in his eyes the next day that he didn't want to hurt her. He loved his little girl. And she loved him.

But she could never trust him.

As a twenty-year-old, my friend spent over a year in a mental hospital. Later she became a nurse and worked as a medical missionary on a Navaho Indian reservation. When she was in her fifties, she married an eighty-year-old invalid. He died, and now my friend is a widow, getting by on social security and a little babysitting.

My friend has tried to tell her brothers what happened in her childhood. She wasn't blaming their dad; she just wanted understanding. But they didn't want to hear. Now she counsels a bit with other women who were sexually molested by their fathers in childhood.

She's not bitter.

She even believes God has used her pain to shape her character and teach her many important things. She speaks of her dad now with deep compassion.

But my friend too, like the children of alcoholics, never had that important growing up time of puppy love.

Her dad, a person she had to trust, let her down.

Woititz lists a number of characteristics of adult children of alcoholics. They're generalizations, and not every characteristic will fit. But they do portray what happens when parents seriously let their children down.

Woititz says that adult children of alcoholics:

- Guess at what normal behavior is.
- Have difficulty following a project through from beginning to end.
- Lie when it would be just as easy to tell the truth.
- Judge themselves without mercy.
- Have difficulty having fun.
- Take themselves very seriously.
- Have difficulty with intimate relationships.
- Overreact to changes over which they have no control.
- Constantly seek approval and affirmation.
- Usually feel they are different from other people.
- Are super-responsible or super-irresponsible.
- Are extremely loyal, even in the face of evidence that the loyalty is undeserved.
- Are impulsive; they tend to lock themselves into a course of action without giving serious thought to alternative behaviors or possible consequences. This impulsive behavior leads to confusion, self-loathing, and loss of control over their environment.*

In another book, *The Adult Children of Alcoholics Syndrome,*[†] counselor Wayne Kritsberg charts emotional, mental, physical, and behavioral characteristics of adults who grew up in alcoholic homes (see page 119).

What all this means is simple.

It's one thing to have some salesman who is a stranger let us down. It's one thing to have a friend we trust turn against us. It's one thing even to have a preacher we trust let us down.

But when mom and dad let us down, it's another thing entirely. It's not just a question of alcoholism, though

---

* Extracted from Woititz, *Adult Children of Alcoholics.*
† (Pompano Beach, FL: Health Communications), 1985.

| CHARACTERISTICS OF PEOPLE FROM ALCOHOLIC HOMES | | | |
Emotional	Mental	Physical	Behavioral
Fear	Thinking in	Tense	Crisis
Anger	absolutes	shoulders	orientation
Hurt	Lack of	Lower back	Manipulative
Resentment	information	pain	behavior
Distrust	Compulsive	Sexual	Intimacy
Loneliness	thinking	dysfunction	problems
Sadness	Learning	Gastrointesti-	Inability to
Shame	disabilities	nal disorders	have fun
Guilt	Hypervigilance	Stress-related	Strong desire
Numbness		behaviors	to fit in
		Allergies	Compulsive-addictive disorders

that's a common problem. A child who grows up in a home where he or she cannot trust mom and dad—for whatever reason—will probably be scarred for life.

I remember a preaching mission I carried out one Easter in a large Lutheran church in Minneapolis. For some reason or other, I spoke of my own childhood in an illustration. I was blessed as a child, growing up in a small Michigan town in the home of loving Christian parents, with a dozen aunts and uncles living only a few miles away. I spoke of this and of what I had experienced as a child.

After the sermon, a well-dressed businessman about forty years old came up to me. "I'm so angry at you," he said.

I had my puppy years.

He had not.

And, he continued, "It just isn't fair."

He was right, of course. It isn't fair. It isn't fair for some to have loving childhood homes and for others to grow up in homes marked by fear and uncertainty.

What's more, there's no easy explanation as to why God should permit it.

I know. Christian theology says that the injustice and pain in society is a result of sin, not of God's action. And this is true. We human beings are not only sinners; we are also victims of the sins of others. God didn't make your home a hell.

But he did permit it.

And that's what is so hard to understand. That's why so many adults whose parents let them down cry out, "If God is so loving and all-powerful, how could I have been put through such pain as a child?"

There is no real answer for this question.

But there is hope—the hope that God will act to redeem not only our past, but our present and future as well. The hope that God will act to repair the damage and to make us whole.

What steps can you take to undo the damage done to you by parents who violated your trust and let you down? Here are three:

(1) *Express your emotions to God.* Nearly everyone who has been betrayed by mom or dad represses emotions. This leads, among other things, to a terrible sense of isolation. We feel we don't dare let our true feelings be known, and we even hide them from ourselves.

But God loves us enough to accept us as we are. You need never be afraid to tell him how you feel. Even if you are angry at him, as are most children whose parents let them down, you can express that anger freely and be sure God will never strike out at you nor reject you.

The psalmists understood the anger we sometimes feel against God. They express what many "good" Christians try to hide—feelings of abandonment, resentment, loneliness, and hurt. Look, for instance, at these words from Psalm 102:

My heart is blighted and withered like grass;
  I forget to eat my food.
Because of my loud groaning
  I am reduced to skin and bones.
I am like a desert owl,
  like an owl among the ruins.
I lie awake; I have become
  like a bird alone on a roof.
All day long my enemies taunt me;
  those who rail against me use my name as a curse.
For I eat ashes as my food
  and mingle my drink with tears
because of your great wrath,
  for you have taken me up and thrown me aside
  (vv. 3–10).

Do you see it?
The psalmist *blames God!*
He explores his feelings and lets God know just how he feels.

Yet the psalmist does this in the context of faith. Later, in the same Psalm, he reminds himself and his readers that the Lord "will respond to the prayer of the destitute; he will not despise their plea" (Ps. 102:17). We can trust God so much that we can even be angry with him.

If you are someone whose parents have failed you, this is the first thing you need to do to find healing. You need to look within, to identify the anger and the hurt that comes when those you have to trust let you down. You need to bring those feelings out of the dark spaces inside where you try to hide them and share them with the one Person who truly understands.

The one Person who will accept you and your emotions completely.

The one Person whose touch can bring healing and release.

(2) *Rebuild your self-image.* The puppy-love years are important because they shape much of our view of ourselves. In the ideal home, love is freely given, and mom and dad let us know in a million little ways how important we are to them.

But in too many homes love doesn't work that way. When mom or dad's life revolves around a bottle or some other kind of personal obsession, the children are pushed aside, ignored, or even abused. The message that comes across to the child in a million little ways is how *un* important he or she is.

Mom and dad did not affirm her importance.

Now she can't feel important at all—not even to herself.

Yet it is to this very point that God speaks to us in a firm, loving voice. God speaks in Creation, saying by that act in which he shared with humankind his own image and likeness, "You are important—and important to me." God speaks in Covenant, saying in his promise to bless all the peoples of the earth through Abraham, "You are important—and important to me." God speaks in Christ, saying to humankind and to you and me through the sacrifice of his Son, "You are important—and important to me."

Whatever your parents may have said or done, *God* affirms your importance.

God affirms your worth and value.

God affirms, in Creation, Covenant, and especially in Christ, that you are loved.

The second step toward healing is to take those affirmations and make them your own.

You need to get up every morning, look in the mirror, and using your own name say,

"I, Karen, am loved."

"I, Karen, love myself."

"I, Karen, know that God loves me."

"I, Karen, deserve love."

There are other affirmations you can make, too. Affirmations not based on empty hopes, but on the fact that God not only loves you but is active in your life.

"I, Karen, can accept my feelings."

"I, Karen, can express my feelings."

"I, Karen, can control my appetite today."

"I, Karen, can listen sensitively to others."

"I, Karen, can teach that Bible study."

"I, Karen, can make good decisions."

"I, Karen, can risk sharing with a friend."

"I, Karen, *can!*"

Self-effort? Not at all. Simply an affirmation of faith in truths that are taught in God's Word. Even without a personal relationship with Christ, God loves you. Now, with that personal relationship with Jesus established, you are not only loved—you are enabled!

Listen to what Paul says: "I can do everything through him who gives me strength." See those first two words?

I.

Can.

Whatever your childhood was like, however the loss of puppy love may have affected you, you are not trapped. Christ has set you free. Now at last you can affirm with the Word of God, "*I can* do everything through him who gives me strength" (Phil. 4:13).

(3) *Change.* This may seem threatening, but it is the necessary third step to repairing the damage done when childhood trust is violated. You and I need to take responsibility for our own actions now and not act as we were programmed by our parents to act.

Yes, we need to learn to identify and express our feelings. Yes, we need to work on the way we look at ourselves. But we need to do more. We need to recognize unhealthy patterns in our behavior and consciously, purposefully change.

Think back over that list of thirteen characteristics of adult children of alcoholics offered by Woititz. Do you, for example, have trouble following through on a project from beginning to end? Next time you're tempted to abandon a project, say "No!" And keep on that project until you're done.

Do you constantly seek approval and affirmation from others? Next time you do a good job, don't tell anyone. Look at it as your secret, and tell *yourself* what a good job you did.

Are you impulsive, jumping into things without thinking them through? Next time you feel you just must act *now*, determine to wait. If you are ready to tell off your boss and quit your job, write the letter of resignation— but don't give it to your boss until at least a week has passed and you've had time to think it all over.

I know. A lost childhood is something you can never, ever recover. You probably won't know puppy love until you dash, all fresh and new, into God's presence. Then, I suspect, you'll find what you miss so terribly. You'll find that offering and receiving of love freely and easily. That scampering, somewhat mischievous, playful, carefree quality that comes when a little child is in the presence of a daddy who loves him or her completely.

But until that time comes and your childhood is recaptured in God's presence, you *can* find healing and renewal. You *can* express your pain to God. You *can* take his Word for how important you are. And, enabled by his loving Spirit, you *can* change.

You *can* still become what you might have been if only you'd had a mom and dad you could trust.

And, God bless you!

For Meditation and Discussion

1. If this chapter is about you, look over the lists of characteristics quoted from Woititz and Kritsberg. Talk about what you've discovered with your spouse or a close friend. Or share the lists with a loved one and ask which characteristics they see in you. If you want to buy one of these books, each is published by Health Communications, Inc., 1721 Blount Road, Suite #1, Pompano Beach, FL 33069 and can be ordered for you by your local bookstore.

2. Write out a prayer, a psalm, or even a letter to God telling him your feelings about missing out on a puppy-love childhood. Don't hesitate to express your feelings honestly. God not only will listen; he'll help those feelings change.

3. Memorize verses, such as Philippians 4:13, that affirm your "I can" capabilities in Christ. Verses to consider include: Exodus 14:13; Isaiah 41:10; Joshua 1:9; Ephesians 1:19–20, 3:17–18, 3:19–20.

9

Not a Matter of Trust

When Andy and Joan got married, they seemed to have everything going for them. They had dated for two years and spent a lot of time planning their life together. Each had a good job. They were doing all right financially, and they were even able to buy a little house that was well within their budget.

But when Andy and Joan came to see a counselor, they were close to divorce. Joan was in tears, and Andy was tight-lipped and tense.

The reason? Joan wanted a baby. And so, without telling Andy, she had quit taking birth control pills.

When Andy found out, he was furious. For one thing, he didn't think they were ready for the financial responsibility—after all, they had a house to furnish. But what really bothered him was that Joan would do something like that without consulting him. How could he ever trust a wife who would deceive him in something so important? For months now, Andy had hardly spoken to Joan, much less shown her any affection.

Joan was hurt and angry, too, and she also felt deceived. She desperately wanted a baby; she'd told Andy that before they married. She was in her thirties and intensely aware of the ticking "biological clock." Besides, Andy had said he wanted a baby, too.

Andy's answer to that one was a classic: "Sure, we talked about having a baby. We also talked about buying a boat."

I like to read the "Can This Marriage Be Saved?" feature in the *Ladies Home Journal*. Every time the magazine is delivered to our house, I grab it before my wife can get her hands on it. Every once in a while, some couple mistakes me for a marriage counselor and asks me to meet with them, so I need all the help I can get!

And I got a lot of help from reading about Andy and Joan in the September 1987 issue. Their situation was so, well, typical. Each was positive the partner he or she had trusted had let him or her down. But in a way, the problem wasn't one of violating trust at all! It was a problem of communication.

Each had a clear mental picture of his or her own priorities, and each thought the other understood those priorities.

So when Joan's actions went against Andy's priorities, he was hurt and angry. And when Andy wouldn't take action on Joan's priorities, Joan was even more hurt.

Each thought the one person that could be trusted most had let him or her down. But what really happened was that neither really understood the mental picture of their life together that the other had constructed. Neither one really understood the other's priorities.

That is what the counselor in the *Ladies Home Journal* pointed out. He observed that Joan and Andy had confused talking with communication and daydreaming with planning. We might add that they also confused "someday" with commitment.

I suspect that very often when we feel hurt and think that someone we've trusted has let us down, the problem is one of communication rather than trust. We talk. We have a clear mental picture of what we mean. And we simply don't realize that the other person not only may misunderstand, but may even have a different mental picture entirely.

Joan wants a baby—now.

Andy wants a baby, too—someday.

Andy wants to furnish the new house—now.

Joan wants to furnish the new house, too—someday.

Joan is worried because she has heard that the older she gets, the more problems there might be with the pregnancy. She's even told Andy in rather general terms that a mother's age is a concern.

But Andy never thinks of Joan as "old," and he simply isn't aware that Joan is close to that "dangerous" age. And Andy is totally unaware of Joan's growing anxiety and fear.

Joan stopped taking birth control pills because she thought they'd agreed to have a baby. Now she feels Andy is reneging on their agreement and cannot be trusted.

Andy was hurt and angry because he thought that talk about babies, like the talk about a boat, was daydreaming. So now Andy backs away from intimate relations because he interprets Joan's stopping the pill as untrustworthy behavior. He's too anxious and upset to make love. What if she does it again?

What an unnecessary tragedy! Two people in love, two nice people, each of whom is convinced he or she can't trust the other.

Yet the problem isn't one of trust at all.

It's a problem of communication.

A problem of misunderstanding.

Before you read on, stop a minute and think. Think about times when someone you trust has let you down. Then ask yourself: Is it possible I *misunderstood?* Did he or she really know my priorities? Did he or she understand my feelings? Was he or she really aware of what I wanted or what I intended to do?

And ask yourself this: Did I really know his or her priorities? Did I understand his or her feelings? Was I aware of what he or she wanted or what he or she intended to do?

If your answer to many of these questions is no, then perhaps you need to reevaluate. Perhaps the person you trusted didn't let you down after all. Perhaps he or she just didn't understand.

Thinking over past hurts really can help. If what others have done was not a violation of our trust, but a result of misunderstanding . . . well, that changes things. We hurt less. We find it easier to forgive. We're willing to try again, to trust even though we thought we'd never trust again.

Yet the most important thing about the story of Andy and Joan is that it can help us avoid future hurts. If we learn the lessons taught by their experience and apply them, we may save ourselves and others unnecessary pain. And we may discover that others—our spouse, our children, our neighbors, our friends, our fellow church members—are more trustworthy than we supposed!

What are the lessons we need to learn? Well, let's look to the Apostle Paul for some good communication habits that can save and nurture your trust relationships.

Each of these communication suggestions is drawn from the fascinating Book of 2 Corinthians. In this most personal of his epistles, the Apostle was writing to a church full of problems. Earlier Paul had written a letter of advice, telling the Corinthians how to deal with the cliques, immorality, lawsuits, and other issues dividing the local Christian community. But many in Corinth had rejected Paul's advice, and they had said cutting, painful things about Paul himself. So in 2 Corinthians Paul was writing to reaffirm his love for the Christians of Corinth and to strengthen the trust relationship, which some had violated and others had accused Paul of violating.

Second Corinthians contains many wonderful truths. But one of its most significant values is found in studying how the Apostle communicates. Paul takes pains to avoid any misunderstanding of his thoughts, feelings, expectations, intentions, and motives. The patterns we see in Paul's letter help us identify some good habits of communication that can help nurture trust relationships:

(1) *Take the risk of sharing your thoughts and feelings, even if you think others are hostile.* Quite simply, if others do not know what we think or feel or want, they won't be able to take these things into consideration when they act. If we're hurt and say nothing, the other person can't say "I'm sorry." And then our hurts fester rather than being healed. Besides, not sharing at all isolates us from others.

Many Corinthians were actively antagonistic to Paul, yet he writes, "We have spoken freely to you, Corinthians, and opened wide our hearts to you" (2 Cor. 6:11). By taking this initiative Paul invited open communication from the Corinthians. He knew their negative attitude, but he also knew that if trust were ever to be reestablished, he must take the lead.

Paul goes on, "We are not withholding our affection from you, but you are withholding yours from us. As a fair exchange—I speak as to my children—open wide your hearts also" (6:12–13).

Building and strengthening trust relationships takes

just this on our part: opening our hearts and speaking freely to others.

(2) *Include feelings when you "speak freely" to others.* If you fall into the habit of hiding your real feelings, then the "inner you," will remain unknown. People will feel uneasy because they sense that somehow they don't really know who you are. People will wonder how you feel about them and their actions. Without feedback on how you feel about what they say and do, they will never know quite how to act around you. And they won't know how to determine your actions.

Joan, for instance, never told Andy about her fears, so he couldn't take those fears into account when looking at their situation. All he could see was her actions and her words, which without the underlying emotions seemed incomprehensible and uncaring.

Even when Paul's authority as an apostle was attacked by some in Corinth, he shared feelings that showed him to be human and vulnerable. He says, "We do not want you to be uninformed, brothers, about the hardships we suffered in the province of Asia. We were under great pressure, far beyond our ability to endure, so that we despaired even of life. Indeed, in our hearts we felt the sentence of death" (1:8–9).

It was a risk to share such feelings of despair and discouragement—emotions that might even be used against him. But Paul said, "We do not want you to be uninformed." He knew that if others were to trust him, they must know him as he really was. He knew that if others were ever to share their feelings with him, he must take the lead by sharing his.

So Paul does share feelings, often: "I still had no peace of mind" (2:13). "We were harassed at every turn—conflicts on the outside, fears within" (7:5). "I am glad" (7:18). "I am afraid . . . that your minds might be led astray" (11:3). And there are many other passages like these.

When we regularly include information on our feelings in our talk with others, they will come to understand who we are, and trust will grow.

(3) *Be very clear on how you perceive issues. Don't leave room for misunderstanding of your actions.* When people don't know how you view a situation, they won't understand what you do. If they see things differently, misunderstandings may become serious.

For example, Andy withdrew because he perceived Joan's actions as untrustworthy. Neither was able to explain why he or she acted as they did. It took a counselor to help Andy realize that Joan saw her actions simply as following through on something to which they had both agreed.

Paul was careful to explain how he saw the situation in Corinth and why he had acted as he did. He said, "We do not write you anything you cannot read or understand. And I hope that . . . you will come to understand fully" (1:13).

To make sure the Corinthians understood fully, Paul carefully explained his actions: "I made up my mind that I would not make another painful visit to you. . . . I wrote as I did so that when I come' I should not be distressed by those who ought to make me rejoice. . . . I wrote you out of great distress and anguish of heart and with many tears, not to grieve you but to let you know the depth of my love for you" (2:1–4).

Often the feeling that someone you trust has let you

down is relieved when that person explains exactly how he saw the situation and why he acted as he did.

(4) *Express your expectations clearly and specifically.* Even those who do consider your feelings and perceptions may let you down if they don't understand what you expect them to do. But when people understand what to do to satisfy another's needs or expectations, trust can be rebuilt.

That is why it's important to think through what you really want in a particular situation. Be very specific, defining just what the other person might do that would meet your needs, then let him or her know your expectations.

Paul took pains to specify to the Corinthians just what he expected from them. "I urge you, therefore, to reaffirm your love for [a sinning brother who has repented]" (2:8). "Each man should give what he has decided in his heart to give, not reluctantly or under compulsion, for God loves a cheerful giver" (9:7).

This lesson about clarifying expectations was one Andy and Joan had to learn before their situation could improve. Each knew that the other was hurt and upset, and each felt trust had been violated, but neither knew what he or she could do to satisfy the other's needs or to restore trust.

The counselor helped them here, urging them to tell each other exactly what they wanted. Joan wanted to start a family before the risks increased with age. Andy wanted them to make plans together with more concern for financial security. Joan and Andy finally agreed that they would hold off on buying furniture and that they would have a baby next year when Andy felt more secure financially.

Others can live up to your expectations only when you make those expectations clear.

(5) *Let others know ahead of time what you intend to do.* If they object, you can talk it over and work out something that will be mutually satisfying. But if you don't send up advance warning, your actions may come as an unwelcome surprise and even be viewed as a violation of trust.

Joan didn't think she needed to tell Andy she was going off the pill. After all, she thought he wanted a baby, too. Because she acted without telling Andy what she intended to do, their marriage was almost destroyed.

Paul was clear in stating his intentions to the Corinthians. "I already gave you a warning when I was with you the second time. I now repeat it while absent: On my return I will not spare those who sinned earlier or any of the others." The Corinthians may not have liked to hear the warning. But there was no doubt about what Paul intended to do when he returned. Any action he took then couldn't be seen as a violation of trust.

Trust grows when we are open and aboveboard.

(6) *Use communication skills to serve others, not manipulate them.* When we use any skill to get our own way rather than to serve others, our motive will be recognized sooner or later. Others will come to see us as selfish and uncaring. They will not trust us, and they soon will resist doing what we want. In the end, a selfish use of any skill is self-defeating.

When it comes to communication, we would all do well to examine our own hearts and motives. God gives us relationships with others not just so we can get our own needs met, but so that he can use us to meet their needs, too. God calls us to serve others and minister to them. When good communication skills are wedded to a ministry motivation, all will be blessed by the trust relationships that develop.

This too is reflected in 2 Corinthians and in Paul's life. "It is for you," Paul said of his ministry (5:3). "I will very gladly spend for you everything I have and expend myself as well" (12:15). "Everything we do, dear friends, is for your strengthening" (12:19).

If Paul's attitude is ours, the trust relationships we so desire will come. For you and I will be people whom others truly can trust.

For Meditation and Discussion

1. Identify one or two times when someone close to you, someone you trusted, has let you down. Think back over that situation carefully. Is it possible that what really happened was not so much a violation of trust as a failure in communication? If so, how does that affect your feelings about the incident? About the person or persons involved?

2. Think carefully about your own communication patterns. Do you have any of the bad habits identified in this chapter? Which relationships do these habits most affect? Plan now what to say or do to improve communication in that relationship.

3. Would you agree or disagree with the following statement? Why?: "The most important thing we can do to build trust relationships is to focus on our own motives and on how we relate to others. It's not a matter of finding someone else who is trustworthy. It's a matter of being trustworthy ourselves."

10

Bright Hope

Earlier in this book I shared my candidate for worst hymn. So at this point it seems only fair to share a favorite. It's a hymn called "Great Is Thy Faithfulness." As I was planning this chapter, the tune kept coming back to me, with a particular phrase from the third verse.

I suppose you're familiar with the hymn. It's been a favorite in all the churches I've attended during my fifty-six years. It's a true celebration hymn, with the first verse celebrating God himself and the third the blessings we have through a personal relationship with him.

> Great is Thy faithfulness, O God my Father,
> There is no shadow of turning with Thee;
> Thou changest not, thy compassions they fail not;
> As Thou has been Thou forever wilt be. . . .
>
> Pardon for sin and a peace that endureth,
> Thy own dear presence to cheer and to guide;
> Strength for today and bright hope for tomorrow,
> Blessings all mine, with ten thousand beside!

And then comes the refrain,

> Great is Thy faithfulness!
> Great is Thy faithfulness!

Morning by morning new mercies I see;
All I have needed Thy hand hath provided—
Great is Thy faithfulness,
Lord, unto me.*

Yet it's hard to celebrate the faithfulness of God when someone we trust has let us down.

It's hard when morning by morning, instead of new mercies, we face new heartbreaks.

But there's one passage of Scripture that offers us cause to celebrate no matter what tomorrow morning may bring. It's a passage that not only gives us the secret of strength for today, but offers us a bright hope for tomorrow.

To understand it, we need to return for a moment to the first century and to feel what the Apostle Paul must have felt as he sat down to write yet another letter to the Corinthians.

If anyone had reason to be discouraged, it was surely Paul. Those Corinthians! Always bickering. Ready to fight over doctrine, but also ready to ignore open sin in the fellowship. Judgmental. Misinterpreting the Spirit's gifts as indications of who is "more spiritual" rather than using them to serve one another in love. Disorderly in worship. Turning the Lord's Supper into an occasion for carousing. No wonder the apostle had written in his first letter that these believers behaved like "mere men"— not like Christ's people at all!

Such problems might be overlooked in spiritual infants. But Paul had been with the Corinthians for what some think was three years, and he'd sent others to instruct them. And for some reason the members in this church still did not respond and grow.

---

* "Great Is Thy Faithfulness," by Thomas O. Chisholm. Copyright 1923, renewed 1951. Hope Publishing Co., owner. Used by permission.

They ignored Paul.
Some ridiculed him.
Many were sullenly rebellious.
Who was he to tell *them* what to do?

If you've ever had such treatment from someone close to you, someone you care about, you can understand Paul's feelings. You know what it's like to be ignored, to face ridicule or sullen rebellion. You know what it's like to merit love and trust, but to have the person you care about let you down. Paul's agony is something you can understand—as I can.

It's hard then to understand some of the words Paul wrote in this situation. In fact, when I first noticed them, I wondered. Is Paul completely honest here? Has he resorted to flattery? Is this manipulation?

I wondered because I just couldn't see how Paul could possibly mean it when he wrote, "I have great confidence in you; I take great pride in you. I am greatly encouraged; in all our troubles my joy knows no bounds" (2 Cor. 7:4). How could Paul be honest and still write to members of this church, "I am glad I can have complete confidence in you" (2 Cor. 7:16)?

Could I write this if I were in Paul's place?

How could I ever say something like this to persons who had let me down again and again?

I found the answer in a theme that runs through this New Testament letter, specifically in an explanation that Paul offers us in 2 Corinthians 4:16–5:21. This is a long passage, but let me quote it, italicizing the keys to Paul's thought:

> Therefore we do not lose heart. Though outwardly we are wasting away, yet inwardly we are being renewed day by day. For our light and momentary troubles are

all. So *we fix our eyes not on what is seen, but on what is unseen. For what is seen is temporary, but what is unseen is eternal* (4:16–18).

In the next passage (5:1–10), Paul pauses and looks far ahead. Upon our death, he writes, the mortal in us will be "swallowed up by life," and we will be at home with the Lord. Sure of this ultimate transformation, we make it our goal on earth to please God. Standing in awe of God, then, and sure that the future he promises is real,

we try to persuade men. What we are is plain to God, and I hope it is also plain to your conscience. We are not trying to commend ourselves to you again, but are giving you an opportunity to take pride in us, so that you can answer those who *take pride in what is seen rather than what is in the heart.* If we are out of our mind, it is for the sake of God; if we are in our right mind, it is for you. For *Christ's love compels us,* because we are convinced that one died for all, and therefore all died. And *he died for all, that those who live should no longer live for themselves but for him who died for them and was raised again.*

So from now on *we regard no one from a worldly point of view.* Though we once regarded Christ in this way, we do so no longer. Therefore, *if anyone is in Christ, he is a new creation;* the old has gone, the new has come! *All this is from God, who reconciled us to himself through Christ* and gave us the ministry of reconciliation: that God was reconciling the world to himself in Christ, not counting men's sins against them. . . . *We are therefore Christ's ambassadors,* as though God were making his appeal through us. We implore you on Christ's behalf: Be reconciled to God. God made him who had no sin to be sin for us, *so that in him we might become the righteousness of God* (5:11–21).

Think with me as we break this vital passage down and look at its central teachings:

(1) *"What is seen is temporary."* Everything that we can touch, see, feel, or experience in this present world is caught up in the process of change. We can be positive of one thing—nothing stays the same. In contrast, there are eternal things, outside of time, that do not change. These are things we can count on always.

When we suffer because others we trusted let us down, we need to follow Paul's advice and fix our eyes on the unseen, not on what is seen. If we focus only on what others are like *now*, we're sure to become discouraged and lose hope. We need to look beyond what people are like now, to catch a glimpse of what they can become.

(2) *"Take pride in . . . what is in the heart."* Paul now explains that his expressions of confidence are not an effort to manipulate or "commend ourselves to you." It is just that Paul takes no pride in what is seen. His concern is "what is in the heart."

All too often we focus only on what the people we love say and do. Paul looks ahead to a future which does not depend on present behavior but on the heart. Simply put, if Christ is in the heart and life of our loved one, that Presence is a basis for hope.

(3) *Christ's love compels.* "Compel" does not mean to cause change by external force. It means to motivate change from within. Only the love *of* Christ, which stimulates love *for* Christ, can motivate a real change in anyone. You and I might cause others to change their behavior by arguing, crying, or threatening. But real change in persons comes as a love response to the love which God offers us in Christ.

It is a tragic mistake, if we have been hurt by someone we trusted, to try to force change. Sometimes we might produce an unwilling change in behavior. But we would also produce resentment.

God's way of love is designed to produce willing change, change which has no tragic side effects.

(4) *Live for him.* Paul now expresses a profound truth. The purpose of Christ's death for us was to work an inner transformation, so that all who live in him "should no longer live for themselves but for him who died for them and was raised again." Jesus endured the cross to put an end to our selfishness and to refocus our lives on God. And those who truly live for Christ are people we can trust truly to care for us.

Notice Paul says that God's *purpose* at Calvary was to create a people who will live for him. So Paul, confident that nothing mere human beings do can thwart the purpose of a sovereign God, is sure that even the Corinthians will come to the place where they surrender their selfishness and begin to live for Christ! Paul can have "complete confidence" in the Corinthians, not because he sees evidence of transformation in their behavior, but because he knows that Christ is in their hearts and that the purpose for which Christ died will surely be accomplished.

(5) *We regard no one from a worldly point of view.* The only basis of evaluation that people of the world have is observation of what goes on in the material universe. They might well look at the Corinthians and ridicule. Those folks *Christians?* Feuding. Immoral. Disruptive. Judgmental. Ha!

But think for a moment. From a worldly point of view, how does Jesus himself seem? An idealistic dreamer, so out of touch with reality that his own people urged the

Romans to give him a criminal's agonizing death! Yet to us Christians, who see with the eyes of faith, Jesus is the Son of God. The cross was the will of God, undergone for our salvation. And death was not the end, but simply the prelude to resurrection for Jesus, and for us.

The world judges only by what can be seen—those changing, shifting, ever-different images that conceal rather than reveal reality. Faith teaches us to look beyond what can be seen to what is eternal. And we who see Jesus clearly are called to look at others just as clearly. We are not to see others as they are, but as they one day will become because of Jesus.

(6) *"If any man be in Christ, he is a new creation."* Or, as Paul wrote, "The old has passed away; the new has come."

The newness may not yet be reflected in behavior. The person we love and trust may still let us down. But deep within the heart of the believer, God has planted his new life, creating him or her anew. Because the new has come, the new will surely sink its roots deep within the heart and, in God's time, bear fruit.

(7) *God . . . reconciled us to himself through Christ.* The best simple explanation of the powerful theological concept, "reconciliation," is that it means "to bring into harmony." You listen to the radio, and when the time is announced, you "reconcile" your watch by matching radio time. God has acted in Christ to bring us into harmony with himself. He has done this through the death of his Son and the gospel proclamation that, because of Jesus, God does not count our sins and does not hold them against us.

The transforming power of the Gospel is summed up in the *forgiving* love of God in Jesus Christ.

He does not count our sins.

He does not hold them against us.

And in the gospel God calls us to bring our lives into harmony with him.

(8) *We are . . . Christ's ambassadors.* Now Paul reveals how he views himself and even other Christians. We are ambassadors, entrusted by God with the transforming message of the gospel. We are sent to speak of, and to embody, God's forgiving love. We are to display that powerful love of God which can motivate men and women to change from within, and which results in bringing their lives into harmony with God.

This verse has often been taken as a call to Christians to convert the unsaved. But Paul is not writing here about pagans, but about Christians. Christians who need to bring their lives—their thoughts and actions—into harmony with who God is. So this "ministry of reconciliation" God gives us is a ministry to believers, a ministry intended to help others become in daily life what they already are as Christ's people.

How do we minister in a life-changing way? We do it by *expressing the forgiving love of God to those who have hurt us.*

We do it by not counting their sins. We don't say, "this is the fifth time you've been late!" Or, "this is the twenty-seventh time you've criticized me in front of my folks."

We do it by not holding their sins against them. Oh yes, we let others know when something they do hurts. But then we forgive, and we let the forgiving love of God wipe away our grudge, even as it wipes away the other person's sense of guilt or shame.

We let people respond to love willingly.

We never try to make people respond unwillingly by anger, antagonism, or threats.

(9) *In him we . . . become the righteousness of God.*
Paul bases his confidence on God's unseen work in human lives rather than on others' present behavior. "God made him [Christ] who knew no sin to be sin for us, so that in him we might become the righteousness of God." Here we see again the stated purpose of our sovereign God. Jesus took on our sin "so that" in him we might become righteous.

What we see in the present life of our loved one, or what we see in our own life just now—these things are simply the "seen." They are temporary and passing. What is real and true and steadfast may be unseen now, but if we or our loved ones have a personal relationship with God through Christ, we can look ahead with confidence.

We *do* have a bright hope for tomorrow.

God is at work within the heart of every believer and, in his time, each one of us will become righteous, like our God. And, since "God is not willing that any should perish" (2 Pet. 3:9, KJV), we also have hope for the non-Christians we care about.

So Paul was being totally honest when he wrote, "I have great confidence in you." He was being completely sincere when he said, "I am glad I can have complete confidence in you."

Paul *was* confident.

Despite the bickering.

Despite the overlooking of sin.

Despite the judgmentalism.

Despite everything.

Paul was confident, because he knew that with Christ in the heart, every individual's future is bright with hope.

It's the same for you and me. Even when a person we care about and trust lets us down.

Despite the hurt.

Despite the betrayal.

Despite the insensitivity.

Despite even repeated violations of our trust.

If Christ is in the heart, the future of persons who betrayed our trust is bright too.

It may be that we need to pause for a moment on that thought. *Their future is bright with hope.*

This is, I suppose, a book for people who have been hurt by someone they trusted. As such, perhaps I should end it with words of comfort—words that minister to you.

Instead, I'm ending with a challenge. I encourage you to minister to the person or persons who let you down.

You see, you *are* one of Christ's ambassadors, entrusted with that forgiving love of God which brings reconciliation with God and reconciliation between persons. To fulfill that trust, you and I both need to follow the example of the apostle Paul and communicate to our own "Corinthians" the confidence which Paul's letter exudes. We need to see our hurt, not just as a pain to be borne, but as a cry for help. Then, with Christ's own love, we need to reach out again.

We need to let the other person know:

I'm not counting your sins.

I'm not holding them against you.

Instead, I have complete confidence in you.

Jesus, in your heart and mine, is real. And Jesus in the heart truly is hope for glorious things to come.

With this confidence, even when we are hurt, we can lift up our hearts with our voices and sing,

> Pardon for sin and a peace that endureth,
> Thine own dear presence to cheer and to guide;

Strength for today and bright hope for tomorrow,
Blessings all mine, with ten thousand beside!

Great is Thy faithfulness!
Great is Thy faithfulness!
Morning by morning new mercies I see;
All I have needed Thy hand hath provided—
Great is Thy faithfulness,
Lord, unto me.

For Meditation and Discussion

1. A pastor friend of mine says that nine-tenths of his ministry is to have confidence in his people until they are able to have confidence in God. How much difference does it make, when you fail, if someone encourages you with a "You'll make it. Good for you!" rather than a "You let me down *again!*" How do you think each response would make you feel? What impact would each have on your future efforts to please that person?

2. Think through the nine points drawn from 2 Corinthians 5. Which most helps you put in perspective the times you have been let down by someone near you? Talk about each of these concepts with a friend, and see if he or she selects the same concept. Discuss not only your choices, but the experiences your selections brought to mind.

3. This chapter suggests that being let down by someone you trust may be a call to minister to him or her. Whom do you think God might be calling you to serve, as his ambassador, with the reconciling message of God's forgiving love in Jesus?